CRETE:
OFF THE BEATEN TRACK

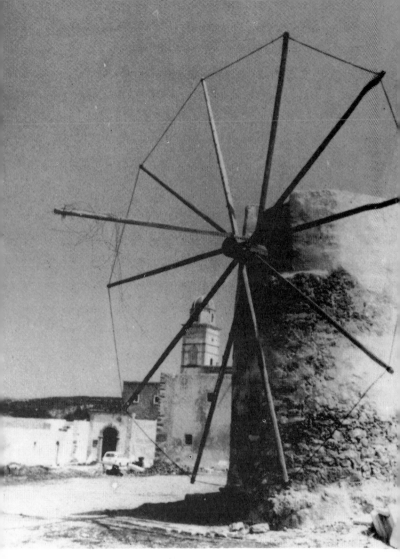

Toplou Monastery and windmill in eastern Crete.

CRETE:
OFF THE BEATEN TRACK

A GUIDE TO COUNTRY WALKS
AND MOUNTAIN HIKES

BRUCE & NAOMI CAUGHEY

CICERONE PRESS,
MILNTHORPE, CUMBRIA

ISBN 1 85284 019 6

Homer the Odyssey

Book XX

"Out in the dark blue sea there lies a land called Crete, a rich and lovely land, washed by the waves on every side, densely populated and boasting ninety cities. Each of the several races of the island has its own language. First there are the Acheans; then the genuine Cretans, proud of their native stock; next the Cydonians; the Dorians with their three clans; and finally the noble Pelasgians. One of the ninety towns is a great city called Knossos, and there for nine years, King Minos ruled and enjoyed the friendship of almighty Zeus . . ."

CONTENTS

INTRODUCTION

Most visitors to Crete have lofty expectations about an island culture that conjures up magnificent images and sets Greek mythology in motion. Crete seldom disappoints the traveller, but to experience the island fully is to stray away from the cities and resorts. The days of supertourism are here to stay and with it comes a certain passivity towards the surrounding culture. Walking allows anyone in almost any physical condition a means to participate in the island's dynamic history.

The ruins of ancient civilizations have combined with the forces of nature to create an atmosphere ripe for exploration. The treasures of the heartland can be unlocked by taking an hour-long ramble to an abandoned monastery, a day trip to a Minoan palace, or a strenuous trek into the upper reaches of the Lefka Ori (White Mountains).

The most satisfying aspect of each excursion are the people you meet along the way. The true Cretan spirit is undaunted in the small villages and mountain hamlets. The hospitality you will surely encounter is aggressive at times, but always from the heart. It is as if you were a time traveller back among the daily life of the ancients. No longer is your day fragmented by routine and the clock. What becomes important is the changing of the seasons, the rising and setting sun and the cycle of the moon.

We have tried to satisfy various tastes and endurances in compiling this guide. The walks encompass the unique facets of life past and life present on Crete. From the hundreds of footpaths criss-crossing the island, we have narrowed down the myriad of choices to only the most interesting and beautiful. The goal of this guide is to become a sort of Ariadne's thread to lead you through the labyrinth of possibilities during any stay.

What began as a two month sabbatical from corporate jobs ended as a year-long odyssey into backcountry Crete. Shortly after our arrival on this remote Greek isle, my wife and I set out to explore the untouristed south coast by foot. Without enough fresh water we stumbled upon the Roman ruins of ancient Lissos (Walk 11) during a trek from Sougia to Paleohora. After a thirsty return to the city, we tried to satiate our curiosity over the site that "we alone" had re-discovered. The seed was planted and we didn't leave until after experiencing over 100 country walks and mountain hikes of which the very best are shared in these pages.

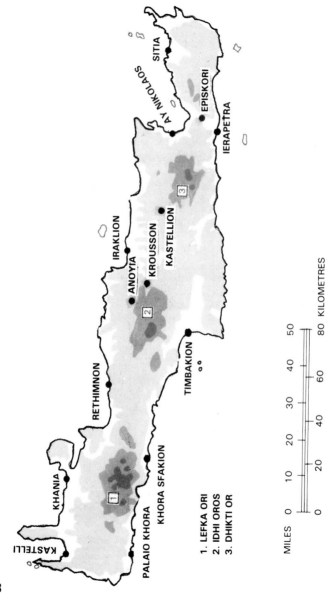

8

WHAT THIS BOOK CAN DO FOR YOU

To be sure, there is a wealth of information contained in this book and a wide range of walking tours to choose from. Some of the longer tours will require that you camp out; others cater to those after a short jaunt with a view or perhaps a coastal trek to a lonely beach. A section on short walks will identify tours of under two hours and will point the way to prime picnic spots. We have made an effort to integrate the unavoidable history of Crete with its extreme natural beauty.

While being careful not to skew the contents towards any one subject, there is a variety of topics covered. In addition to trying to capture the general feeling of each walk, our account covers the flora and fauna one may encounter and a descriptive portion to keep you on the right path. To accompany mere words are a host of visual reinforcements: charts, graphs, diagrams and maps. The photographs should speak for themselves. While attempting to keep the weight of the book within reason, there are special sections on: island dimensions, beaches, flora, fauna, agriculture, weather, safety, comfort, and of course, history.

The walks are organized in three regional sections (west, central and east) for ease in planning an itinerary. Each route and its corresponding walk number are depicted at the beginning of each section.

Once on the trail we have relied more heavily on walking times than distances in kilometres. The logic of this will become apparent when you are face to face with widely differing trail conditions, and elevation changes. Please read the following outline to ensure safe and happy outings through the proper use of this guide.

Time and Topography Chart
This chart is most useful in deciding at a glance if the walk is compatible with your strength and inclinations. It is a quick overview of the relationship between elevation changes (vertical axis) and the average time it takes for a person to cover the terrain (horizontal axis). The landmarks noted within the chart coincide with the overhead map, in effect adding a third dimension.

Landmark Map
An overview of the general direction of the path, the major features

of the terrain and the main landmarks along the way.

Walking Time
Simply the average time it takes a person to complete the walk.
   This carefully estimated time is figured without stops – please allow for them.

Access
Directions to accompany a road map in reaching the beginning of each walk from the closest major city. Also included are the frequencies of bus and boat service in the area and journey time.

Description
The first paragraph of each description is an overview of the entire walk. Any unique landforms and historical aspects are summarized to help you decide among the walks before setting out. Subsequent paragraphs provide useful information while on the trail. We have been careful to note major landmarks in this section to keep you on the correct path.

Language Note
We have always used commonly used transliterations for place names, but the spelling varies widely on maps and signs throughout Crete. When a Greek word is used within the text it will be italicised, with the English counterpart following in parentheses. A few frequently used Greek words will not be followed by the English translation (e.g. kafeneion = cafe, taverna = restaurant/tavern).

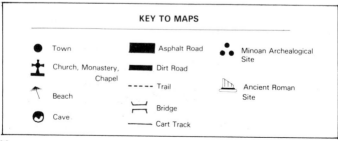

KEY TO MAPS

● Town	Asphalt Road	Minoan Archealogical Site
Church, Monastery, Chapel	Dirt Road	
Beach	Trail	Ancient Roman Site
Cave	Bridge	
	Cart Track	

GENERAL INFORMATION

Access to Crete
There are charter flights during the season May-October from most UK airports to Iraklion (Heraklion) and from Manchester/Gatwick to Hania (Chania).

Scheduled year round services fly to Athens from Heathrow, Manchester and New York with onward flights to Crete.

Details of times and prices are available from all travel agents.

Island Dimensions
A full third of island Greece is represented by the "big island" of Crete. Located in the eastern Mediterranean, Crete is roughly equidistant between Europe, Asia and Africa. It is this strategic location among the commercial sea routes that secured the development of a unique culture. The unfortunate costs, in human life, resulted from the repeated attacks of conquering powers.

Crete is 260 kilometres long with a width that varies from 56 kilometres to 12 kilometres at its narrowest point. The long slender island forms a manifest boundary between the Aegean and Libyan Seas. There is, however, a natural linking with Europe because of the many harbours along the north coast. By contrast, the majority of the south coast is a wall of cliffs to the Libyan Sea, with no major natural harbours and very few outlets.

It is difficult to reflect on any area of Crete without including a backdrop of high mountains. The limestone massifs have altered the history and development of the island by virtually cutting off one area from another. They are central to the undeniable Cretan character and are impressive in their own right. There are 4 principal mountain ranges that dominate the landscape.

1. West   White Mountains (Lefka Ori)
              High Point: Pachnes (2452 metres)
2. Centre   Ida Range
              High Point: Psiloritis (2456 metres)
3. East   Lassithi Range
              High Point: Mount Dikte (2148 metres)
4. Far East   Sita Mountains
              High Point: Afendis Kavoussi (1476 metres)

In addition to the ever present mountainous terrain, Crete is an island of plains and valleys. The fertile plain of Messara is the largest

lowland area on the island with dimensions of 50 km. × 10 km. Isolated at higher altitudes, are the smaller upland plains of: Omalos, Askifou, Nida, Lassithi, and Katharos. These alpine plateaus are most often used as farmland or as summer pasture.

The Omalos plateau is connected to the Libyan Sea by the magnificent Samaria Gorge. Samaria is by far the longest fissure in an island of many gorges and ravines. Caused by excessive bending of the rock strata, these impressive landforms provide some of the most beautiful hiking terrain on Crete.

Other attractions are the island's numerous caves, in every conceivable dimension and location. The caves are linked inexorably with the long history of the island, beginning with the Neolithic cave dwellings. Their uses were expanded to Minoan burial places, cult worship of mythological figures and more recently, hiding places from occupying powers.

Maps
Walking maps for Crete are less than satisfactory.

A general contoured map of Crete is the Nelles map at 1:200,000. and there are similar scale road maps.

The Karta Nomos published by the National Statistical Office at 1:200,000 covers Crete in 4 sheets:
Sheet 16 Iraklion
　　　31 Lasithi
　　　40 Rethymni
　　　49 Chania
Relief is shown in hipsometric tints with contours at 200m, but the names are only in Greek lettering.

N.B. Transliteration from the Greek alphabet often results in various English spellings for place names.

The Greek Alpine Club have issued some 1:50,000 maps for mountain areas of Greece but these have not so far included Crete. The large scale military maps are not available to the general public.

All these maps are available from Stanfords, 12/14 Long Acre, Covent Garden, London SC2E 9LP. Tel: 01-836 1321.

Village scenes - an arched doorway is situated next to a chicken coop while the foreground is composed of a wooden donkey saddle, an olive press mat, and a newly added electricity meter.

Beaches

Crete has a wide variety of beaches in every shape and design. This most tempting landform entices visitors to stretch out, relax and enjoy a cool swim. For those that desire a beach within a city setting, Rethymnon is blessed with a wide girth of white sand on its eastern flank; on the southwest end of the island is the slightly reddish island beach of Elafonisi; Sougia offers a wide rocky beach surmounted by high mountains; a bit to the east is Sweetwater Beach with its fresh water pools; there is palm lined Limni Beach and the popular palm beach of Vai; 8 kilometres of white sand guard the west end of the Messara Plain and Koutsounari has a quiet stretch of glistening black pebbles.

Many of the north coast beaches are now lined with resort hotels. There are, however, plenty of less crowded offerings. We put forward several walks to some of Crete's finest and lesser known beaches. See walks 5, 6, 7, 8, 10, 11, 12, 13, 22.

Flora

The climate and contrasts on Crete provide for a rich assortment of flora to be seen throughout the island. The physical isolation of Crete has fostered the existence of over 100 endemic species and sub-species, out of some 1500 varieties. Early in the year the island is literally covered with a wealth of wildflowers, until the dry summer heat loosens their grasp. Highly localized plants will join you during your walks across the island, but there is a conspicuous absence of forests. Crete was once veiled with trees, but forests now comprise only 2% of the land space (see footnote on page **62**). Unfortunately, their presence seems to have been replaced by an abundance of thorny and spiky plants: thorny brunet, spurge, thistle and sea holly. These drought resistant plants can be a formidable foe for walkers – hence the sturdy knee length boots worn by shepherds. The sparse forest trees that you will see are cypress, juniper, pine, tamarisk and even palm.

The gorges provide a unique, protected environment for the pink spikes of Cretan Ebony and the delicate white bells of Symphyandra Cretica, both are endemics. The deep ravine above Kato Zakros (walk 22) contains the vulgar looking Dragon Arum, alongside thick bushes of wild pink oleander. The coastal plain just below offers a tropical selection of prickly pear cactus and cultivated banana trees.

Throughout the island are fields of heather and thyme, used extensively for the production of honey. Also spotted over Crete's entirety are flowering bushes of oleander, hibiscus, bougainvilla, and geraniums; red fields of Corn Poppies abound in springtime. The upland plains provide likely sightings of magnificent wild orchids and a distinctive Iris Cretica with its orange stripe on blue. On stony hillsides in late autumn is the unlikely crown of light purple cyclamen. Another mountain variety – Cyclamen Cretici – shows its tender white flowers in the spring.

The smells of fragrant herbs are distinctive to the island. Most important is the classically famous endemic herb of Dittany (locally known as Dictamos). Found along the lofty reaches of Mount Dikte and on sheer rock faces, the herb is widely used to cure ailments and to comfort women during childbirth. Easily spotted herbs on Crete are: marjoram, sage, oregano, thyme, summer savoury, and rosemary.

Fauna

To be perfectly honest, Crete does not have a terribly exciting array of wildlife – with a few notable exceptions. It is the birds and exotically coloured butterflies that provide the most common sights. Small birds on the island include: larks, swallows, goldfinches, and several species of shrikes and warblers. In the mountainous areas near Psiloritis and the Lefka Ori there are many large birds of prey and scavengers. We have frequently spotted vultures, eagles, crows, and buzzards in these higher regions. A large roost of hawks live in the caves that line the Valley of the Dead just below Ano Zakros. In the nearby coastal plain next to the Minoan palace of Kato Zakros, eglets and herons can be seen. On a small island off the Hania coast called Agios Theodoros, there is a colony of rare Elonora's Falcons.

Agios Theodoros and several other off-shore islands also provide sanctuary to the truly unique Cretan Wild Goat – affectionately called "Kri Kri". Their last known natural habitat is the Samaria Gorge. For the past 2 decades it has been strictly forbidden to hunt the nimble goats that are known for their distinctive arc of horns. Other wild mammals known to reside on Crete are rabbit, weasel, marten, bat, badger, hedgehog, and the usual small rodents. While the fish population is limited, harbour restaurants manage to conjure up freshly caught displays of calamari, lobster, red mullet, sardines, swordfish and shrimp.

Agriculture

Despite the primitive agricultural methods that still prevail through-out much of the island, there is a lavish selection of fruits and vegetables in the local markets. Modernization is slow in coming, but

15

The ever present goat will keep you company during your treks about the island.

many tractors and motor driven ploughs can be seen. The use of thermokipos (plastic greenhouses) has vastly improved the export potential of low lying areas, with the production of Europe's earliest tomatoes and cucumbers. Important are the large vineyard tracts in the Sitia and Iraklion districts. They are used for the profitable production of sultana raisins as well as domestic wines. The mainstay of the island, however, remains the olive.

Olives

During your exploration on Crete, you will never be far from aged olive trees that flourish everywhere in the terraced countryside. Young trees take a very long time to mature and are started not from a seed, but from branch cuttings that are carefully planted beneath the soil. The collection of the fruit doesn't allow for mechanisation, making each step of the harvest slow to the unchanging pace of medieval times. In winter, after the olives have sufficiently matured, they are painstakingly harvested. The process begins in late December, and isn't finished until the warmth of spring is upon the island.

Bearing the burden of village life.

Black nets are spread out below the gnarled trees to catch the falling olives. The harvester is forced to hammer at the branches with an unyielding stick to shake the olives loose. The laden nets are then gathered and after the leaves are winnowed out, the olives are loaded into burlap sacks. The procession to the fabrica (olive press) during the winter is a remarkable sight. The villagers load their donkeys, or fill their trucks with brimming sacks after each day's harvest. Inside the fabrica the olives are ground to a pulp before the oil is squeezed out. After the oil has been extracted, the residue is made into soap and the crushed seeds are burned as a cheap fuel.

Weather

After a cool and often wet winter, an early spring comes to Crete bringing a bounty of wildflowers. The colour is everywhere and the island soon appears to be overrun. As suddenly as the flowers appear in mid-March, however, the dry season beginning in May quickly

17

diminishes their ranks. Spring (mid-March – May) and Autumn (September – mid-November) are likely the most pleasant seasons for exploring the island on foot. The days are warm and sunny, but the persistent heat of summer has not yet arrived. There is an occasional gusty day in March, but it is nothing like the Meltemi, the strong hot wind blowing from the north, in August.

For the majority of people who visit Crete in the summer months, there are still many ideal walks. The mountains on the island usually have a cool breeze and the air is noticeably less humid away from the coast. Some of the hikes in the Lefka Ori are possible only in summer – and other walks lead to fine bathing beaches. For those worried about the draining effect of the heat, try a short walk or a picnic.

The topography of the island causes great variations in climate between the south coast, the mountains and the north coast. The temperature is generally higher and more consistent along the south coast, and swimming is possible (though pretty cold in winter) year round. The higher peaks are with snow until late May and the rainfall is considerably higher than on the plains. The north coast experiences cooler, wetter winters, but after a thunderstorm there are crystal clear views to the mountains. At any rate, Crete enjoys more than its share of sunshine – 300 days per year!

Temperature & Rainfall

| Coastal Temperatures | | | Rainfall | | Rainy | Sea Temperatures | |
month	C	F	mm	in	Days	F	C
Jan.	12	54	94	3.7	14	17	63
Feb.	12	54	76	6.0	12	15	59
Mar.	14	57	41	1.6	7	16	61
Apr.	17	62	23	0.9	4	17	63
May	20	68	18	0.7	3	19	66
June	23	74	3	0.1	0	25	77
July	26	78	0	0	0	24	75
Aug.	26	78	3	0.1	0	22	72
Sept.	24	75	18	0.7	2	24	75
Oct.	21	69	43	1.7	5	22	72
Nov.	17	63	69	2.7	8	21	70
Dec.	14	58	102	4.0	13	18	64

Safety & Comfort

We depend on your good sense while taking any of the walks outlined in these pages. While there is the potential for dangerous situations to arise, walking is generally a very safe pastime. The walks in *Crete: Off the Beaten Track* are informal and cover a lot of uncharted ground. Therefore, it is important to know how to use this book along the way (see page 9). Since the walks and hikes appeal to a broad variety of tastes and endurances, it's up to you not to overestimate your vigour. Following are some tips to ensure safe and happy excursions:

– Bring enough water and fruits to avoid dehydration.

– In addition to the food you normally bring, carry some high energy snacks: nuts, raisins, sesame bars . . .

– Sidestep the hottest part of the day to help avoid sunburn or possibly sunstroke.

– Bring sunglasses, hat, sunscreen and lightweight protective clothing. A pair of long pants will also provide protection from thorny shrubbery.

– In case you are caught by darkness, carry a flashlight for a measure of safety. There are occasional caves along the walks that are worth a peek into.

– A small first aid kit and pocket knife are always good to have along. A compass is not essential on all but the longest mountain hikes.

– Carry a current bus timetable to speed connections at both ends of the walks.

– There are a lot of bees (and some wasps) on Crete. Take care around water troughs, fields of heather and thyme, and, needless to say, the many bee hives you will encounter in the countryside.

– There are no dangerous snakes to worry about.

– Yes, Crete has some scorpions. Their bite is painful, but contrary to Cretan folklore, it is not dangerous.

– A poisonous spider called "rogalida" resides on Crete. We've never seen one and chances are you won't either.

– Dogs do their job by raising a fracas as you pass. Usually they are chained to a tree, if not, try to remain unperturbed as you walk on by.

– While walking in a ravine with goats overhead, pay attention to their position, and listen for falling rocks. Don't cover your head

19

with your hands; instead, look where the rock is falling in order to avoid it.

– The sea around Crete is known for its weak currents, but watch for sea urchins under your feet while swimming near rocks.

– If you get lost, try to maintain your calm above all else. Most of the walks are never too far from a village if there is an emergency.

Footwear

Most importantly your footwear should be comfortable and have thick soles. Track shoes may give you nimble footing, but they can leave you with sore feet after longer walks. Ankle support is advisable on some of the rocky limestone paths in the mountains. We found the new generation of lightweight walking boots to be nearly ideal – much cooler and lighter than heavy leather boots.

A couple of suggestions for easier walking: If your toes are stubbing against the front of your boot during long downhill stretches, lace up tighter to hold your foot in place. To prevent heel blisters and get a better grip on the hill, avoid walking on the balls of your feet – walk fairly flatfooted.

Camping

Camping on Crete is not officially permitted outside of designated areas, but . . . If you avoid intruding on someone's private property and camp discreetly, you will likely be left alone. Use your grey matter in selecting from a wide choice of scenic areas both in the mountains and on the coast. Campfires, however, are a bad idea. There is a lack of burnable wood on Crete, and what can burn becomes tinder dry in the summer months.

Transport Alternatives

There are many modes of transport available to the traveller on Crete. So often the question of 'time or money' arises when faced with the alternatives. The access section at the beginning of each walk will assist in deciding the best way to get there and back. Except for the short walks, public transport is often the best way to get around.

Bus

Crete has an extensive bus network that offers reliable, inexpensive transport throughout the island. Bus service is frequent along the main north coast highway, but sporadic on secondary roads. When there is only one bus from the main town to a small village each day, the bus will run to the town in the morning only to return to the village in the afternoon. This schedule is for the convenience of the villagers and the unintended consternation of the sightseer. Though this can be a bit frustrating, the buses are often social gatherings of Cretan villagers that offer colourful glimpses of daily life.

Since more buses run in summertime, the bus timetables are frequently updated. Please obtain the necessary timetables at the bus station for ease in planning your departure and return. We offer approximate bus frequencies and the time of each journey, but will not confound the situation by listing specific timetables that quickly become obsolete. When waiting by the roadside for a bus, don't be shy about flagging it down – it might not stop otherwise.

Car

Most of the walks are accessible by car, (directions can be found in the access section of each walk) but unless you are planning a round trip, a car can be a nuisance. The short walks section, however, is full of possibilities for those who are driving.

It is expensive to rent a car on Crete, but during a limited stay there is no better way to get around. Before setting off, you should be aware of a few things:

– Road conditions on Crete vary widely and are not always accurately depicted on road maps.

– Greek road signs are nearly always followed by English ones.

– Cross the solid white line on the right to allow room when someone wants to pass.

– Blast your horn around blind corners to warn oncoming drivers.

– Roadside shrines are placed as a memorial and a warning that a near-fatal accident has taken place at that location. Please drive safely!

Boat

There are small ferryboats that connect the hard-to-reach areas on Crete during the summer months. There is frequent boat service between the south coast villages at the west end of the island (Chora Sfakion, Loutro, Agia Roumeli, Sougia, and Paleohora) and to several offshore islands. When there are boat connections, we have included them in the access section of each walk.

Another possibility is to rent a sailing or motor yacht during your stay. Since there are small, safe harbours to put in all around the island, it can be a good way to travel. Arrangements should be made before arriving on Crete, at the mainland port of Pireaus.

Taxi

Taking a taxi is often the most reasonable way to travel moderate distances. It is easy to find a taxi in the larger towns and many small villages support at least one. It is a sure sign of value to see so many light grey Mercedes filled with Cretans. They are affordably priced – especially when the bill is split among 4 passengers. Just be certain that the bill is negotiated beforehand with the driver, or that the meter is running. It is quite possible to have the driver return for you, or pick you up at a predetermined time and place.

Motorbike

This is an increasingly popular way to get around Crete on a budget. All of the north coast cities and resorts have rental shops and new shops are springing up in less frequented areas as well. There are many road hazards on Crete that can be dangerous on a motorbike (especially those with a short wheelbase), stay alert!

* * * * *

Some people expressed lament over the influx of debeautifiers that this book might bring to the previously hidden wonders of Crete. In response, we pictured the hiker as non-littering, considerate and able to preserve the untarnished character of the countryside and its endearing people. Please live up to your image.

Crete "On" The Beaten Track

Unavoidable, and at times quite pleasant, are those areas of Crete where tourists and travellers alike tend to congregate. The north coast of Crete has become well developed and relatively well organised in recent decades. The largest tourist centres line the north coast from Iraklion in an easterly flow to Agios Nicholaos.

To the west of Iraklion are the most congruous cities in all of Crete. Both Rethymnon (60km. west of Iraklion) and Hania (50 km, further west), while unique from each other, possess their charms from another era – primarily influenced by the Venetians and more recently by the Turks. The cities are alive with vigorous growth and commerce. Rethymnon is the site of the University of Crete, and is widely considered the intellectual centre of the island. Hania derives its strength and vitality from the dramatic wall of mountain (Lefka Ori) that rises just behind.

There are numerous areas on Crete that everyone touring the island should consider visiting. Although Crete has a long and varied history, it is the remains from Minoan culture that are truly unique. Listed below are the principal places from which to gain a first hand understanding of Europe's first great civilisation:

1)   First and foremost is the remarkable collection of Minoan artefacts displayed in the *Archaeological Museum of Iraklion*. It is the finest collection of Minoan art and implements in the world. There is a thorough and attractively illustrated guide to the museum written by its current director. The museum has opening hours Tuesday – Saturday: 08:00 – 18:00. Closed on Monday.

2)   Sir Arthur Evans excavated and partially reconstructed the *Minoan Palace of Knossos* at the turn of the century. Easily reached from Iraklion, it is the largest and most renowned of the Minoan palaces. See page 28 for detailed information. The site is open daily: 08:00 – 19:00 (Sundays 18:00); winter hours: 10:00 – sunset. Buses leave from the harbour bus station in Iraklion every 20 minutes and stop conveniently at Platia Venizelou and Odos 1821 before arriving at the palace site 6 kilometres away.

3)   *The Palace of Festos* looks out over the Messara Plain from a low hill near the base of the tallest peak on Crete, Psiloritis (2456 m). After examining the heavily reconstructed Palace of Knossos, it will be much easier to understand the unaltered layout of Festos. The palace was built in a superb position, with the upper stories looking down over a central courtyard. In 1903, the still undeciphered Festos disk was found on the palace grounds. (Now on display in gallery III of the Iraklion Museum.)

Only 3 kilometres away, along the same ridge to the sea, are the smaller remains of the *Summer Palace of Agia Triada*. The sea, now comfortably in the distance, once rippled up to the foot of the hill on which the palace is built. Agia Triada was richly decorated in frescoes; including a cunning cat stalking its prey, and a lady seated in a garden. (Displayed in the Iraklion Museum.) Summer Hours: Festos 08:00 – 19:00, Sundays: 08:00 – 18:00. Agia Triada: 08:00 – 19:00, Sundays: 09:00 – 19:00, closed Mondays.

4)   Built on a narrow coastal plain near the northern fringe of the Lassithi Mountains is the *Palace of Malia*. Though it has less to offer the visitor, the site is also worth a stopover. It follows the architectural form of the other palaces, with its central court laid out

on the same axis as that of Festos and Knossos. Summer Hours: 08:00 – 19:00 daily, Sundays, 09:00 – 19:00.

5)   One of the most beautiful walks on Crete leads through a deep ravine to the fifth and final Minoan *Palace of Kato Zakros*. Since this palace was originally built during the final Minoan period it is more simple to distinguish the ruins. See pages 133/134 for more detailed information and a palace diagram. The site is open at all hours.

There is already ample information on the tourist centres and resorts of Crete, so we will not expound further in these areas. The goal of this guide is to direct you out of the queue and into the seldom discovered wonders of this remote Greek Isle.

* * * *

A BRIEF HISTORY OF CRETE

I.	Neolithic Era		6000 B.C. – 2600 B.C.
II.	Minoan Era		
	A)	Pre Palatial	2600 B.C. – 2000 B.C.
	B)	Old Palatial	2000 B.C. – 1700 B.C.
	C)	New Palatial	1700 B.C. – 1100 B.C.
	D)	Post Palatial	1200 B.C. – 1100 B.C.
		(Mycenaean Infiltration)	1200 B.C. – 1100 B.C.
III.	Dorian – Classical Greek Period		1100 B.C. – 67 B.C.
IV.	Roman Period		67 B.C. – 395 A.D.
V.	Byzantine Crete		
	A)	Byzantine	395 A.D. – 651 A.D.
	B)	Arab Domination	651 A.D. – 674 A.D.
	C)	Byzantine	674 A.D. – 823 A.D.
	D)	Saracen Arab Occupation	823 A.D. – 961 A.D.
	E)	Return to Byzantium	961 A.D. – 1204 A.D.
VI.	Venetian Occupation		1204 A.D. – 1669 A.D.
VII.	Turkish Occupation		1669 A.D. – 1898 A.D.
VIII.	Rule Under Prince George		1898 A.D. – 1913 A.D.
IX.	Union With Greece – Pre-WW II		1913 A.D. – 1940 A.D.
X.	Battle For Crete/WW II		1941 A.D. – 1945 A.D.
XI.	Post World War II		1945 A.D. – Present

A stone villa overlooks the comparatively modern city of Rethymnon.

Neolithic Era (6000 B.C. – 2600 B.C.)
Crete was first inhabited by the Neolithic people, who arrived by boat between 6000 B.C. and 4000 B.C. Where they came from is uncertain, but their recently discovered art and dwellings exhibit a sense of tradition. We can only surmise about their life from remnants of objects and tools found in their caves and other locations. They constructed major settlements at Knossos, Mallia, Festos, and Agia Triada.

The Neoliths lived in a primitive way with hunting, gathering and fishing providing most of their foodstuffs. Later, they developed a crude form of agriculture and raised domesticated animals. They were able to work copper and create pottery wares, and seemed to have brought the cult of the fertility goddess with them.

Around 2600 B.C. it appears that there was a great migration of nations from Asia Minor to Greece and Crete. The early Minoan society shows influences from Anatolia (Turkey), Syria, the Cyclades, Egypt and Libya. These immigrants heralded the Bronze Age and brought the ability to use the sea for their own benefit. The ensuing years were marked by a fast pace of change as the Neoliths were assimilated into the newcomers' society. Together these peoples intermingled to create a unique culture that archaeologists have dubbed "Minoan".

Minoan Era (2600 B.C. – 1100 B.C.)
There are four distinct periods of cultural development in this era. Together these periods cover 1500 years of history and record the rise and fall of Europe's first sophisticated civilization. Since the Minoans left no literature, a visit to the Archaeological Museum in Iraklion is strongly recommended. There are also some smaller but interesting collections in the Archaeological Museums in Hania and Agios Nicholaos.

A) *Pre Palatial*   2600 B.C. – 2000 B.C.
The major characteristic of this period is the dramatic development of the arts. This period laid the foundation for Minoan art which later reached its apex in 1700 B.C. It takes no formal training to appreciate Minoan art because of its fluid gracefulness and delicacy of design. It instantly appears harmonious, beautiful, and balanced.

The discovery of the potter's wheel refined and enhanced ceramic wares. Other art forms developed, such as: miniature sculpturing, seal engraving, jewellery making, and working veined rocks into vessels and ritual objects. These objects demonstrate trade links between the Minoans and Egypt as well as the Near East.

B) *Old Palatial* 2000 B.C. – 1700 B.C.

Artwork in precious metals, miniature sculpturing, and seal engraving reached new heights. Floral and curvilinear (spiral) patterns replaced the linear motifs of the Pre-Palatial period. The double axe motif is an exception because it lasted throughout the Minoan Era. The bull, horns of consecration, snakes and female deity figurines comprise most of the ritual objects or religious symbols.

A numerical system and an early form of Egyptian hieroglyphics are added to the Minoan Society. Through productivity and organisation, a hierarchial society develops; the former clan system correspondingly falters. Wealth and power become concentrated, resulting in the building of the first palaces on top of Neolithic debris at Knossos, Festos, Mallia, and Agia Triada.

Due to Crete's strategic seafaring position, its inhabitants were able to act as middlemen, profiting from increased commerce and trade. Eventually, Crete controlled the sea lanes and indeed the culmination of Minoan culture (New Palatial), a "thalassacracy" (maritime empire) had developed. This control likely contributed to their palaces being built in seemingly indefensible positions and without fortifications. Around 1700 B.C. an earthquake destroyed the palaces. It did little to curtail the development of the Minoan society as new palaces were quickly erected over the old palatial debris. The only known exception is the palace at Kato Zakros, constructed for the first time during the New Palatial period in the grand style of the other palaces.

C) *New Palatial* 1700 B.C. – 1400 B.C.

The art, architecture, language, commerce and trade all reached their peaks during this epoch. Art forms of all kinds are perfected and expanded upon. Stoneworking techniques, having suffered a decline in the previous era (Old Palatial), are revived. The Minoans, renowned for their seal engraving and miniature sculpturing, extended these forms into newer and harder mediums. Gold jewellery, having reached a height in the previous era, continued to decorate men and women of the time. Floral and fauna motifs dominated artistic interpretations. Political and religious symbols were further developed and sometimes even combined. Leopards depicted on ritual vessels and axe handles may have symbolised the religious and political authority of Minoan kings.

Derived from hieroglyphics, the original language of the Minoans, Linear A, made its appearance around 1550 B.C. Since it is still undecipherable, its exact contents are not known. Linear B, a new form of writing may have materialized 100 years later (1450 B.C.), although some experts date it to 1200 B.C. Michael Ventris, from England, deciphered Linear B in 1953 and found that it was used primarily in an administrative sense. Linear B has been linked to early forms of Greek, showing a connection between the Mycenaeans, who later dominated Crete, and the Minoans.

The palace at Knossos[1], was the political and cultural centre of Minoan society. It exhibits a carefully considered design which all other Minoan palaces were patterned after. The entire complex was arranged around a central courtyard with a focus on providing light, water, and drainage to all who lived within. Surely the upper echelons had a better lifestyle than the masses who lived outside the palace.

Several features stand out in the 22,000 square metre complex at Knossos. Of special note are the fresh water pipes that carried water from one storey to another. The flush toilet exhibits a good understanding of hydrodynamics with the speed of the water checked by a series of parabolic curves. Grand staircases led to upper storeys with ceramic light wells added to provide adequate lighting to the lower floors. Colourful frescoes decorated the halls, capturing the lively spirit of the Minoans and exacting the essence of the passing moment. Also depicted, are some traditions and costumes. Although not a matriarchal society, women are shown in aristocratic refinement, enjoying a high status and many freedoms.

Certainly one of the most distinguishing features at Knossos is its legendary labyrinth. Although buried for thousands of years, its existence passed down to us via the Classical Greek myth of King Minos and his Monotaur. The legend is a great adventure linking Cretan dynasties with mythology.

Europe, like many others, managed to attract the favours of Zeus. She became the mother of 3 sons, the oldest being Minos. In time, Minos became King of Crete. To prove his connection with the gods

---

1.   Some 20 years after the discovery of Knossos by Minos KaloKarinos in 1878, Sir Arthur Evans began excavating the palace remains. During the ensuing decades the unearthing and somewhat controversial reconstructions took place. It was the ideas and insight into Minoan civilisation revealed at the site of Knossos, that kindled new archaeological excavations throughout Crete. Most of the major archaeological pieces have fallen into place, though there are, undoubtedly, more finds still to come.

he asked Posideon to send a bull from the sea promising it for sacrifice. The bull was so magnificent that a more ordinary one was sacrificed instead, thus angering Posideon. Posideon then made the bull run mad and moreover, he induced Pasiphae, King Minos' Queen, to conceive an unnatural passion for it. Daidalos, a master craftsman and engineer, helped Pasiphae by concealing her in a lifelike figure of a cow. Consequently, she bore a half-man, half-bull called the Minotaur.

Sometime later King Minos' son, Androgeos, was murdered near Athens. King Minos demanded as part of the peace treaty that 7 young men and 7 maidens be sent to Crete each year where they were shut up in the labyrinth with the Minotaur.

The story continues as Thesus, son of King Aegus of Athens, volunteered to go as one of the youths. Thesus, naturally being quite handsome, attracted the attention of Ariadne, King Minos' daughter. Ariadne managed to give Thesus a sword and a ball of thread so he could kill the Minotaur and by retracing his steps, escape from the labyrinth. Thesus succeeds, but on his way back to Athens he forgot to change the black sails of his boat to white. Upon seeing the black sails, King Aegus leapt into the sea from his castle believing that Thesus had been killed by the Minotaur. Thesus then became King of Attica.

For Daidalos' part as an accomplice, he and his son, Ikaros, were punished by King Minos by being detained on Crete. Daidalos, though ever resourceful, contrived a means of escape by making wings of feathers stuck together with beeswax on which he and Ikaros would fly away. Ikaros flew too high whereupon the sun's heat melted the wax and he drowned in the sea. Daidalos escaped to Sicily where he later met his fate.

D) *Post Palatial*   1400 B.C. – 1100 B.C.
Around 1450 B.C. a terrible disaster once again laid waste to the Minoan centres. The catastrophe, though itself is greatly disputed, heralded the decline of Minoan civilisation. Earthquake, revolution, disease and invasion have all been put forth as possible explanations of the final destruction. Another theory is that the eruption of Thera, the volcano on Santorini, caused a huge tidal wave which destroyed the Minoan settlements. In any event, the few who survived sought refuge in the mountains, creating their own strongholds. They carried with them the Minoan culture and from their outposts were able to prolong the decline and final disappearance of the Minoan civilization.

During the Post Palatial period the Mycenaeans infiltrated the island (1200 B.C. – 1100 B.C.). By the end of the era, the Mycenaeans controlled what was left of Minoan civilisation. During the intervening years many Cretans fought under Agamemnon, a Mycenaean, in the Trojan War. The war was fought near Troy on the Aegean coast in what is now Turkey. The Mycenaean state came to an end around 1100 B.C. when Crete was invaded by the Dorians from northern Greece.

Dorian – Classical Greek Period (1100 B.C. – 67 B.C.)

The Dorians, bearing iron weapons, found themselves in a superior position and quickly brought an end to the Mycenaean state and Minoan strongholds. Under the sway of the new rulers, the local population was reduced to serfdom and Crete was divided into townships. The townships were intensely jealous of one another, leading to 10 centuries of internal strife. This in turn caused Crete to pass into international obscurity.

Dorian achievements include the remarkable city of Lato (See walk 20), located high above the Gulf of Mirabello. Another interesting site is the harbour at Falasarna (See walk 12), now raised above sea level due to local uplift on the western end of the island. The most important city of the age was that of Gortys. Eventually the Dorian cities evolved into Classical Greek city states, leaving behind only relatively minor Hellenistic and Classical Greek ruins.

At Gortys, a formal code of law etched in stone was introduced. Although these laws date to at least 500 B.C., they are surprisingly familiar. The script, read from right to left, is composed of a series of statutes and ordinances relating to citizenship, marriage, divorce, tenure of property and inheritance. The laws divide sharply between the upper class, landowners, serfs and slaves. The upper class was favoured throughout. Most of the offences were punishable by fines or restitution – no barbaric penalties are mentioned.

Roman Period (67 B.C. – 395 A.D.)

Like so much of Europe, Crete became part of the Roman empire – though not without suffering 2 years of siege. Under the unified government of the Romans, peaceful living conditions came to Crete because disputes between warring city-states gradually subsided. In addition, the island prospered as it was on the main Roman trade routes. The Romans left their usual signature of roads, walls, arched bridges, aqueducts, health spas, mosaics, and votive statues.

Byzantine Crete (395 A.D. – 1204 A.D.)

In 323 A.D. the Roman empire was split into East and West. Crete eventually became part of the Byzantine (East) empire. It was a peaceful transition headed by Constantine the Great. During Byzantine rule, building of basilica type churches adorned with fine mosaics and pillars was commonplace.

Byzantine rule was interrupted twice by the Arabs, (651 – 674 and 823 – 961) during which time the island became a pirates' haven and many of the coastal settlements and religious centres were pillaged or destroyed. After 5 major attempts, General Nicephorus Phokus successfully recaptured Crete in 961 to lay the foundation for the second Byzantine era.

The Byzantine empire sent noble families to Crete and soon after a feudal system was introduced. Iraklion became the civil and religious capital of Crete. The Byzantines lost command of the island altogether when Constantinople (now Istanbul) was sacked.

Venetian Occupation (1204 A.D. – 1669 A.D.)

Crete was sold to Venice from the politics that ensued from the dividing of the spoils of the 4th Crusade. Boniface of Monferrat sold Crete for 1000 silver marks on August 12, 1204.

Though the Venetians had legal title to the island, their occupation was met with resistance. First from their rivals, the Genoese, and then from the Cretans themselves. Led by the displaced nobility that remained from Byzantium, Cretans staged a series of revolts and sustained guerilla warfare that lasted 150 years. During this time, villages were burned and patriots were executed. Punishments were brutal, often resulting in dismemberment or chainings in the galleys of the numerous castles built by the Venetians. Venetian rule was not firmly established until 1347 when confiscated lands and freedoms were returned to the upper class.

The Venetians were, however, excellent administrators. They built and maintained public works such as roads, bridges, harbours and aqueducts. The alpine plain of Lassithi was drained and tilled under the direction of Venetian overseers. Several stone warehouses were built in Hania to cater for the large Venetian fleet. Their ships kept the Mediterranean trade routes free of pirates. During this era, the town of Rethymnon blossomed into an intellectual as well as artisans' centre. Both Hania and Rethymnon still retain much of their Venetian style architecture (later influenced by the Turks) in their old harbour districts.

A catamaran moored in the old harbour of Rethymnon.

About this time, the Venetian government began to decline leaving the Mediterranean trade routes unprotected. Turkish pirates began to raid Crete, Cyprus, and the Greek mainland. Venice engaged in a series of wars with Turkey. The fifth Venetian-Turkish war began in earnest on Crete in the summer of 1645 and lasted until 1669.

Turkish Occupation (1669 A.D. – 1898 A.D.)
In June of 1645, Sultan Mohamet IV landed 50,000 men on the west coast of Crete and pushed eastward. Two months later Hania fell, Rethymnon soon followed, and by May of 1648 Iraklion was under siege. For 21 years Iraklion held out by itself while all of Europe looked on with bated breath. Though the French intervened briefly, "the great siege" felled Iraklion. It was captured by the Turks in September of 1669. The next 150 years are referred to as the years of repression, characterized by large scale uprisings and subsequent reprisals.

Unlike the Venetians, the Turkish government did nothing to maintain the economic livelihood of Crete. Despite heavy taxes the infrastructure was neglected; roads fell into disrepair and harbours silted up. Unable to get their products to the markets, Cretans suffered further economic hardships.

Under the Turks, religious persecution was practiced – though directed mainly at the higher echelons of the clergy. Much of the remaining population converted, at least nominally, to the Moslem faith to escape economic discrimination. Non-Moslems were forbidden to hold land and were forced to pay higher taxes.

Following an ill-fated uprising led by Daskaloyannis, a Sfakian, the years between 1770 and 1821 marked Crete's worst period of suffering. In 1821 Crete joined the Greek mainland in revolting against the Turks, only to face Egyptian soldiers called in at the request of the Pashas. Greece proclaimed its independence from Turkey in 1832 and the Great Powers (England, France, Italy and Russia) ceded Crete to Egypt. But by 1841, the Turks were back in control.

Monastery Arkadi is Crete's prime symbol of their struggle for independence. Not unlike the people of Massada, hundreds of Cretan resistance fighters were trapped in the Monastery and under siege by the Turks. As capture became imminent, one of the resistance fighters lighted the powder magazine killing nearly all those inside as well as over a thousand Turkish invaders. (The exact figures vary widely.) This appalling event on November 9, 1866 attracted international attention and sympathy for Cretan liberty from the Turks. Despite this empathy from abroad, Crete remained occupied until 1898 when the Great Powers finally forced the Turks out.

Rule Under Prince George (1898 A.D. – 1913 A.D.)
Although Crete could have been united with Greece in 1898, the Allies balked because Greece was again at war with Turkey. The island was granted autonomous rule under the High Commissioner Prince George, the younger son of the Greek king[1].

During this time, Eleftherios Venezelos, a Cretan, formed a party that vowed to seek union with Greece. Eventually Prince George was forced into early retirement as Eleftherios Venizelos became Prime Minister of all of Greece in 1910. The union of Crete with Greece became imminent.

Union With Greece/Pre World War II (1913 A.D. – 1940 A.D.)
In 1913 after Greece signed a treaty with Turkey, Crete was formally assigned to Greece. Between 1914 and 1940, Crete remained

---

1. The Greek Monarchy was abolished by the military junta in 1967.

relatively peaceful as it was outside the main stream of events. Souda Bay, however, was used as a staging area by the Allies during World War I.

Battle for Crete/World War II (1941 A.D. – 1945 A.D.)

Greece was attacked first by Italy, then Germany came in from the north. Unable to hang onto the mainland, the Greek government withdrew to Crete. On May 20, 1941, the Germans launched an airborne invasion. Though numerous English and Commonwealth soldiers were stationed on Crete, the Germans were able to land 20,000 troops at Melame (near Hania) within two days. Once the Germans held the Melame airport, reinforcements poured in. Italian troops landed at Sitia on May 28th. With the east and the north occupied by the Axis, the Allies quickly withdrew from the Sfakian Coast to the south. Though 14,580 allied troops escaped, 13,000 were either killed or captured. German losses numbered 12,000 – 15,000. Despite the Axis forces numbering some 22,000 during the war, the Cretans waged guerilla warfare from their mountain strongholds with the help of English agents and supplies. After the Germans made their last stand at Hania on May 9, 1945 they left Crete.

Post World War II (1945 A.D. – present)

New struggles emerged for Crete as the retreating German forces left a power vacuum. A few skirmishes erupted, but Crete was spared the grief of civil war that consumed the Greek mainland from 1944 to 1949.

Like Europe, the main task was reconstructing and rehabilitating the land and its inhabitants. Though the process was initially slow, the pace quickened under the dictatorship in the Colonels (1967 – 1974). Development transpired at such a fast tempo, especially in the coastal areas, that quality, harmony and loss of character come into question. Tourism is still the driving force behind the ongoing development of Crete.

Crete is an island overshadowed by its history. The character of the inhabitants, its rugged beauty, sunshine and beaches continue to draw increasing numbers of visitors each year. Like the peak of Psiloritis, Crete takes a different shape from different angles. It seems that part of Crete is suspended in time; the other struggling with the pressures of modernization. While the people can be delicate and gentle, there is an indomitable core, toughened by the struggles that have rocked the island, that will continue to weather the changes to come. Crete's future may well lie in the hidden depths of its past.

At the little-frequented beach of Falasarna

Short Walks

For those interested in a shorter version (usually 1-2 hours) of a longer walk, a tip for a picnic place, or a visit to a lesser known historical site – read on. These shorter walks are often better accessed by car, but some are also easily reached by bus. This listing is simply an outline with place names, walking time, accessability, a brief synopsis and the pages in which to turn for more detailed information plus a map of the area. To quickly find a more detailed account of the short walk, coordinate the hours listed and the page numbers. Similar to the main body of the book, the short walks are arranged geographically, beginning in the west and moving east. Enjoy!

A close look at the intricate Venetian stonework on the facade of Monastery Gouvernetou.

A) Akrotiri Peninsula

Walking time: 1 hour, allow equal time for return.

Access: See page 43.

Synopsis: Stop off at the 17th century Monastery of Agia Triada on the way to the more protected Monastery of Gouvernetou. The walk begins near the intricate stone façade of Gouvernetou, leading down a well worn footpath to the sea. Along the way are two fascinating sites: Little Bear Cave and the impressive complex of the abandoned Monastery of Katholiko.

Picnic Tips: Yes! Near Little Bear Cave or the Monastery of Katholiko.

Detailed Information: See page 45, begin at hour 1.

B) Theriso – Meskla

Walking Time: 2 hours.

Access: See page 46.
Synopsis: A confining ravine provides the only entrance to
Theriso, allowing for a revolutionary attitude to emerge. From this
protected setting Eleftherios Venizelos convened an illegal assembly
in 1905, whose goal was the union of Crete with Greece. The walk
begins in Theriso and tracks along country roads in the foothills of the
Lefka Ori. Ending in Meskla, the lush greenery takes on a thickness
unknown to the rest of the island.
Picnic Tips: Meskla has broad shade trees, running water and
innumerable picnic spots around the outskirts of the village.
Detailed Information: See pages 46-49.

C)   Chora Sfakion – Sweetwater Beach – Loutro
Walking Time: 2¼ hours.
Access: See page 71.
Synopsis: A short coastal walk on a marked footpath begins at the
south coast village of Chora Sfakion. At the midpoint is a cliff
enclosed beach with fresh water just beneath its surface. Soon the
picture perfect village of Loutro, situated around a tiny harbour,
comes into focus. No cars!
Detailed Information: See pages 72-75;

D)   Imbros Ravine
Walking Time: 2⅓ hours.
Access: See page 75.
Synopsis: If the hike down Samaria Gorge sounds a bit long, or a bit
crowded, this walk is a perfect alternative. A good trail drops
gradually through the wild beauty of Imbros Ravine.
Detailed Information: See pages 76-78.

E)   Sougia – Ancient Lissos
Walking Time: 1¼ hours, allow equal time for return or ask for the
boat schedule from Lissos to Sougia (or, on to Paleohora).
Access: See page 84.
Synopsis: The south coast village of Sougia is likely the kind of
place you'll want to stay for more than an afternoon. A wide, rocky
beach is stretched out to the east of town and the views to the Lefka
Ori are beautiful. A marked trail leads up a cleft behind the small
port. It rises quickly up the rugged ravine before coming to a ridge
above Lissos. Drop down into the valley where the Greco-Roman
health centre (asklepieion) once flourished. Lissos is the perfect
place for near solitary exploration of another age.

Picnic Tips: The olive terraces of Lissos provide a picturesque setting for a lingering picnic with views to the sea. Don't forget the corkscrew.!

Detailed Information: See pages 85-87.

F) Falasarna

Walking Time: ½ hour, or longer if you please.

Access: See page 88.

Synopsis: On the far western edge of Crete there lies a series of sandy beaches on a narrow coastal plain. A short excursion along a country track leads to the uplifted remains of a Dorian port. The fascinating area is beautiful and still undiscovered by the multitudes.

Detailed Information: See pages 88-89.

G) Spili – Mourne

Walking Time: ½ hour, allow equal time for return.

Access: See page 91.

Synopsis: Spili is a small, yet thriving mountain village that is at once appealing due to its pleasant setting. In the centre of town, among shops and tavernas, water cascades out of a unique stone fountain. Just 100 metres south of Spili, a small country road passes into rolling hills to the sleepy village of Mourne. Stop and enjoy the pace at one of four Kafeneions that are tucked under leafy shade trees.

Detailed Information: See pages 91-92.

H) Monastery Preveli – Limni Beach

Walking Time: 45 minutes, allow equal time for return.

Access: From Rethymnon centre, follow Dimitrakaki Street (next to the National Garden) out of town. Continue south before exiting right towards Koxare on the main Plakias route (22 kms.). Drive through the Kourtaliotiko Gorge, and turn left at Assomatos. Before reaching Lefkogia, turn left onto another paved road (32 kms.). Continue past the abandoned, lower monastery, finally reaching the Monastery of Preveli (37 kms.).

After visiting Preveli, backtrack on the same paved road for about 2 kilometres. Turn right on a dirt road (it merges along a wide curve) that leads downhill to a parking area just above the trail to Limni beach.

Synopsis: This excursion begins at the historic Monastery of Preveli, located in a barren setting high above the south coast. After a short drive, a marked trail leads down a steep hillside to the palm beach of Limni. Situated at the base of a narrow ravine, this oasis is easily superior to Vai in terms of beauty and isolation. Limni beach permits nudism.

Picnic Tips: There are some wonderful, shaded spots just below Monastery Preveli facing the Libyan Sea. The abandoned lower monastery is also a pleasant setting. For an unlikely Taverna lunch walk (or swim) just 15 minutes to the east of Limni Beach. The footpath is moderately difficult.

Detailed Information: See pages 95-96, hours 3 – 4¾.

I) Thronos – Monastery Arkadi

Walking Time: 2 hours.

Access: See page 96.

Synopsis: The village of Thronos presides over the fertile Amari Valley, but is itself imposed on by the vast limestone face of Psiloritis (2456 m). This walk winds its way through a rural setting, ending at the fortified Monastery of Arkadi. On November 9, 1866, the Venetian stonework of the monastery was nearly destroyed by an explosion that had reverberations around the world.

Picnic Tips: There are towering pine trees near Arkadi that would provide just the right setting.

Detailed Information: See pages 97-101.

J) Amari Valley Frescoed Churches

Walking Time: 2 hours.

Access: See page 102.

Synopsis: The Amari Valley has a hidden trove of frescoed churches. An easy walking loop visits a couple of them, while wandering among orchards of cherry, apple, pear and fig trees. The dominant peaks of Kedros and Psiloritis provide a compelling backdrop for the excursion.

Picnic Tips: There are literally endless possibilities in the Amari Valley. The area in front of Agios Ioannis Theologos is nice for a respite, but for a lovely picnic, try the wooded area below the village of Amari.

Detailed Information: See page 102.

K) Lassithi – Dikteon Cave

Walking Time: 1 hour.

Access: See page 111.

Synopsis: An excursion into the rural way of life on Crete begins at the small town of Agios Georgios, along the ring road of Lassithi. The town is home to a good folklore museum which provides a fine beginning for the walk across the windmilled plain. Track along next to Venetian irrigation channels before climbing uphill, to a fabulous view of the ancient lake bed. The walk ends at the mythological birthplace of Zeus.

Picnic Tips: The best places are near the perimeter of the plain. We found a nice shaded spot just south of Mesa Lassithi – take a look around.

Detailed Information: See pages 111-114.

L) Limnes Loop

Walking Time: 1½ hours.
Access: See page 114.
Synopsis: Not far from the modern hotels of Agios Nicholaos, narrow stone towers emerge from above the trees allowing cloth sails to harness the energy of the wind. The windmills are only a small, but integral part of the rural lifestyle that Limnes has preserved from the past. This short walk rambles along country roads to the nearby villages of Houmeriakos and Vrises before circling back around.

Picnic Tips: There is a cool and shaded seating area beside the Monastery Kermaston with a view to the valley below.

Detailed information: See pages 114-118.

M) Kritsa – Panagia Kera – Lato

Walking Time: 1 hour, allow equal time for return.
Access: See page 118.
Synopsis: The village of Kritsa enjoys a panoramic view over the Gulf of Mirabello from its mountainside position. There is an old way of life that exists alongside the handicraft shops that dot the main street. Beginning in Kritsa, the walk soon leads to the richly frescoed (14th and 15th centuries) church of Panagia Kera. A country track then leads through fields of olives to the impressive Dorian ruins of Lato.

Picnic Tips: With its marvellous views and flat grassy places, the area around Lato is perfect for a picnic – or a sunset.

Detailed information: See pages 118-122.

N) Mochlos – Venetian Tower

Walking Time: 1 hour, allow equal time for return.
Access: Take the main north coast road in an easterly direction from Agios Nicholaos towards Sitia. After 41 kms. you will reach the

small town of Sfaka. On the west side of town take a rough, small road leading down to Mochlos 7kms. away.

Bus service is frequent to Sfaka from either Agios Nicholaos or Sitia. A taxi may be hired for the trip to Mohlos and back to the bus stop.

Synopsis: Dropping into Mochlos along a poorly kept road there are superb views over the soft contours of the coastal plain. The walk begins at the small village of Mochlos just across from a tiny island that once housed a Minoan settlement. The flat country road follows the coastline to the east through plots of loquat and lemon trees and various types of produce. The walk ends just before a wall of rock cliffs at a Venetian watch tower built alongside a whitewashed chapel.

Picnic Tips: The last 15 minutes of the walk is loaded with picnic possibilities. Try a place just above the coastal road.

Detailed information: See page 128. hours 1½ – 2½.

O)   Kato Zakros – Valley Of The Dead

Walking Time: ½ hour to 1½ hours depending on how far you walk into the ravine. Allow equal time for return.

Access: See page 130 . Follow the directions to Kato (Lower) Zakros.

Synopsis: This fascinating excursion begins at the recently disco-vered Minoan Palace of Kato Zakros. It was built on a hillside near the sea and the unearthing has provided some of the richest and most interesting archaeological finds on Crete. From the site, walk away from the coast on a dirt road before turning right (next to some thick banana groves) onto a path leading up the ravine. It is a good, marked trail that parallels the dry stream bed, at times merging with it. Once surrounded by the dramatic rock walls of the "Valley of the Dead", it is not difficult to imagine the Minoan burials that took place in the caves along the upper reaches.

Picnic Tips: There are shaded areas on the hillside opposite the palace site – nice views! However, you may want to try some charbroiled fish at one of the tavernas along the beach road.

Detailed information: See pages 131-132, begin at hour 2 for a description of the palace.

Patched cloth sails are unfurled during the drying heat of summer in Limnes.

Country Walks
& Mountain Hikes

NB: The times given are accumulative.

1) AKROTIRI PENINSULA

Walking Time: 2 hours from the Monastery of Agia Triada. 1 hour from the Monastery of Gouvernetou (Allow equal time for return.)

Access: Follow Venizelou Street out of Hania in an easterly direction. Approximately 6 kms. outside of Hania, turn right at a sign indicating the town of Kounoupidiana. 12 kms. outside of Hania, turn left at a sign indicating Agia Triada – ½ km. more to another marked left turn. Follow the small tree lined road to the gates of the monastery.

Bus Journey Time: ½ hour.
Only 1 bus in the late afternoon goes as far as Agia Triada. If you don't have your own transportation, a taxi is a viable alternative. (There is an inexpensive set fare to the airport; it's only a 3 km. walk from there to the monastery.)

Description: The peninsula of Akrotiri is full of varied natural splendour and areas of historical interest. The area is still noted for its abundance of wild game and a large portion of central Akrotiri is reserved as a hunting ground. One of the finest day trips from Hania lies just 16 kms. away, beginning at the Monastery of Agia Triada, and continuing along the road to the north. The area is packed with historical treasures that can be seen during the moderately easy 2 hour walk to the Monastery of Katholiko.

The Monastery of Agia Triada (Holy Trinity) was built into a sheltered position by two monk-priest brothers in the early 17th century. It is a fine example of a monastery from the era of Venetian

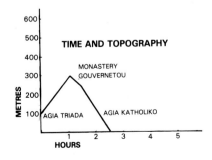

43

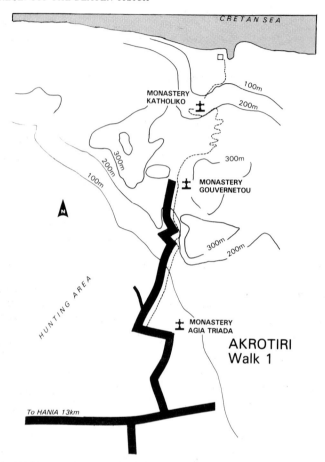

CRETAN SEA

100m
200m

MONASTERY
KATHOLIKO

300m

300m

200m
100m

MONASTERY
GOUVERNETOU

N

300m
200m

HUNTING AREA

MONASTERY
AGIA TRIADA

AKROTIRI
Walk 1

To HANIA 13km

rule (1204 – 1669). Inside the courtyard proper, there are well tended gardens accented by graceful stone archways. The church, now perfumed by years of burning incense, was built in the style of the Italian renaissance. Perhaps the most distinguishing aspect of the church are the finely carved wooden pews that line the sanctuary. Today the monastery is the Orthodox Seminary; however, decreasing numbers of young Cretans seem to be interested in the priesthood each year.

In front of Agia Triada is a good road leading west from the parking area. At a "T" intersection follow the sign to the right (north), through a protective ravine to the Monastery of St. John of Gouvernetou. This isolated Monastery was built in the 16th century and is well known for the intricate Venetian stonework that lines the church's façade. Unfortunately, much of the church's upper reaches were destroyed by fires set during the Turkish occupation. Since rebuilt, the church has retained much of its original character. Just inside the entrance, is a painting of St. John the Hermit who lived below in a cave near the Monastery of Katholiko. The work is nearly covered with small silver plates (simulacra), each one representing people or parts of the body that the petitioner wants cured. Behind the altar, in a small room, is a particularly fine icon of the Virgin Mary. The surrounding stonework somehow survived the wrath of the Turks. (1h).

After Monastery Gouvernetou, continue north towards the sea on a well worn footpath to two fascinating complexes. The first is called Arkoudospilia (Little Bear Cave), just 15 minutes down the trail. It is a large natural cave that derives its name from a rock within that was said to resemble a sitting bear (an abstract one at best). At the cave's entrance is a small chapel.

On down the trail, the unexpectedly impressive complex of the Monastery of Katholiko is stretched out below. The trail evolves into steps as an array of buildings set across a narrow riverbed comes into better view. In 1741 Tournefort wrote of Katholiko (*Voyage into the Levant*), recalling the "descent of 135 steps cut in the rock among terrible precipices" adding that "it has so often been rifled by the Corsairs, that they let it run to ruin". Although it has been centuries since African pirates forced out the last of the monks, the remaining structures bring accolades to another era. The bridge spanning the ravine contains a solitary cell previously used for the imprisonment of sinning members. The flat top of the bridge is easily wide enough for two cars to pass, but it leads only into mountain walls. The huts along the far side of the ravine were used as hermitages. St. John lived in a nearby cave just above the monastery. Each year on October 7th hundreds join in a pilgrimage from Gouvernetou to Katholiko. (2h).

The riverbed may be followed through the sparsely forested ravine to a small rocky inlet about 20 min. away. A small boat house once used by the monastery and some building foundations are the only man-made remains at the water's edge. (2h 20m).

2) THERISO – ZOURVA – MESKLA

Walking Time: 2 hours.

Access: Take the coastal road west from Hania towards Kastelli. After 3 kms., turn left at the sign indicating Theriso. The paved road leads through a spectacular ravine before arriving at the village of Theriso (17kms.).

Bus Journey Time: ½ hour.
There is a morning and afternoon bus from Hania to Theriso. At this time they run only on Monday, Wednesday and Friday.

It may serve you well to consider hiring a taxi for the short ride.

Return: There are 3 buses daily from Meskla to Hania. If you find yourself waiting for an afternoon bus, think about the 5 km. walk to Fournes. Buses run from Fournes to Hania every 1½ hours until early evening.

Description: "The inhabitants of this upland district are a hardy and fine race of Cretans, partaking in all the independent spirit and bearing of the neighbouring Sfakiots, but with less of their lawless propensities." In 1865, Captain Spratt offered this glowing account of the residents of Theriso. Beginning in Theriso is an idyllic ramble through three well grouped mountain villages. The walk stays on country roads that track along the green slopes at the base of the Lefka Ori.

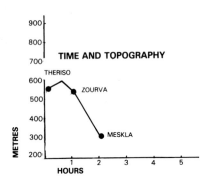

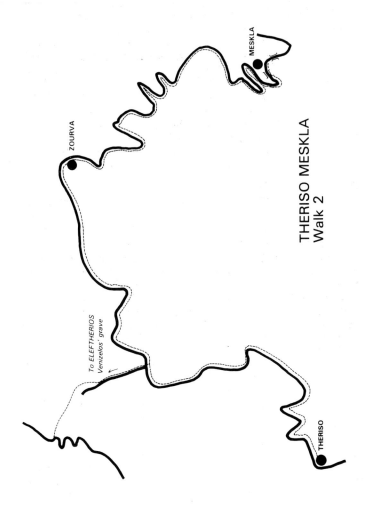

THERISO MESKLA
Walk 2

MESKLA

ZOURVA

To ELEFTHERIOS
Venizelos' grave

THERISO

Thanks to a confining ravine that provides the only entrance to Theriso from the north coast, the small village became a famed stronghold. The protected location was used extensively by guerrillas in the long struggle against Turkish rule. Just seven years after the Turks left Crete, Eleftherios Venizelos convened an illegal revolutionary assembly in Theriso. Its primary aim was to seek union with Greece. This well educated lawyer gained stature when the union became close at hand. In 1910 Venizelos was named the Prime Minister of Greece. Union of Crete with Greece followed shortly afterwards in 1913.

Near a grouping of shaded tavernas, a small museum with period photos follows Venizelos' turbulent political career. Incidently, he remains such a revered figure in Crete that his bespectacled portrait still hangs in most kafeneions – regardless of the owners' political inclinations!

On the south side of the village is a small double naved chapel with a huge shade tree inside the walled courtyard. A cement road just in front leads uphill (away from Theriso), soon turning to dirt. Stay on this small track as it brings you to a ridge overlooking a deep valley, and back to Theriso. The road crosses to the opposite side, shortly returning to another view of Theriso. In ½ hour, the road reaches an intersection along the same ridge. Here there is a water spigot with a tin cup hanging on the back of the nearby signpost. Do not turn left, but continue straight on (west), after a cool drink. (½h).

It is another ½ hour of mostly downhill walking to the tiny village of Zourva. The road persists next to a sheer rock face, while offering a wide vista to the lush country below. Zourva is built on a knoll and surrounded by deep folds created by the geomorphic upheaval of nearby mountains. Many of the stone houses have once whitewashed ovens on their vine-covered verandas. Some of the more dilapidated dwellings now serve as animal pens. The infrastructure consists of a kafeneion and a bent water tap located next to a chapel as you leave the village. That is the simple beauty of the area. (1h).

The road winds downhill around the knoll, through well tended kipos (gardens) and sporadic clusters of pine forest. The superb view up to Lakki, with its blue domed church, is dominated by the naked face of the Lefka Ori from behind. In less than an hour, the red tiled roofs of Meskla create a vivid tableau against a garden of green. The village prospers from the orchards that extend far from its fringe. There are a couple of tavernas and near the bus stop is a place to rent a room for the night. On the far side of town are the 14th century frescoes of the Church of the Transfiguration. The running water and

Right: View from above, of the abandoned Monastery Katholiko.
(Walk 1)

cool shade trees leave a lasting impression on the visitor, but to stumble onto the village festival[1] was absolutely unforgettable! (2h).

Just beside the cathedral as you enter Meskla is a large terraced area with a small stream running through the middle. We couldn't help but notice the quantity of karpusi (watermelon), beer and wine chilling in the water. A festival in the making!

We returned later in the evening to a crowd of hundreds. Most were from Meskla and the surrounding villages. The atmosphere was friendly and soon the night air was filled with [over] amplified strains of Cretan music. After the second course of roasted lamb, the dancing began in earnest. The circles of intertwined dancers were overshadowed by the acrobatic steps of the brostaris (leader). Jumping and spinning while slapping the sides of his boots, the brostaris captured the vitality of the moment while demonstrating his manliness. The mark of a successful party didn't come until the wee hours, as the participants drew their pistols and rattled off rounds into the moonless sky.

3) CROSSING LEFKA ORI

Walking Time: 15 hours in 2 or 3 days.

Access: Bus Journey Time: 1 hour.
There is bus service from Hania to Omalos 4 times daily.

Return: From Anopoli to Chora Sfakion, there is one early morning bus. An expensive local "taxi" may also be arranged for the ride down. There is bus service 4 times daily from Chora Sfakion to Hania.

If leaving from Loutro – there is boat service to Chora Sfakion in the summer 3-4 times daily. See walk 8 for a beautiful 2 hour walk along the coast to Chora Sfakion.

Description: "On entering the gulf of Khania I was struck with the grandeur and beauty of the White Mountains, which well deserve the name bestowed on

---

1.   During the summer months there are many festivals in the smaller Cretan villages – usually honouring a saint, a harvest or a patriotic event. Keep a watch on the kafeneion windows for posters advertising the when and whereabouts. The north coast cities sponsor their own brand of festival on a larger scale. Check at the Tourist Office for any current information.

Left: Tucked away in a garden of green, at the base of the White Mountains, is the village of Meskla. (Walk 2)   **49**

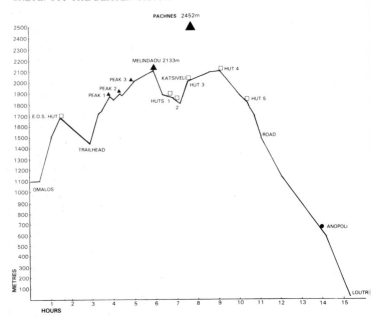

them by both ancients and moderns . . . The fame of the Cretan Ida is greater than that of these snow clad summits, and I had some difficulty in persuading my companions that the majestic forms before us were not those of the loftiest and most celebrated mountain(s) in the island."

Robert Pashley – February 8, 1834

The quote by Robert Pashley should prompt any avid hiker to consider this trek. The Lefka Ori (White Mountains) offer a most striking landscape from afar, but hiking through their interior is the only way to learn their desolate secrets – for they hold many.

Before arriving at the flat, upland plain of Omalos you should be prepared for a strenuous 2-3 day hike. It should only be attempted in summer as adverse weather – rain, snow and resultant run off – would make the trail impassable in the cooler months. To make the trip more pleasant and safe, we recommend bringing along the following items:

50

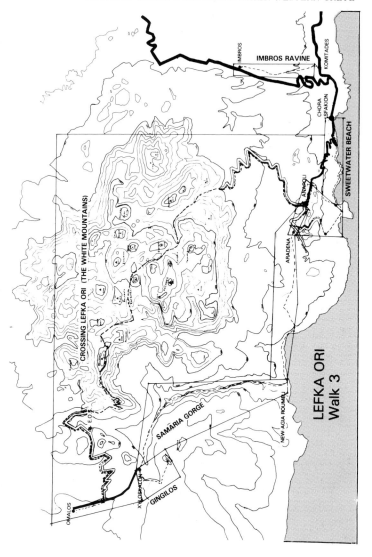

IMBROS RAVINE

IMBROS

KOMITADES

CHORA SFAKION

SWEETWATER BEACH

ANOPOLI

CROSSING LEFKA ORI (THE WHITE MOUNTAINS)

ARADENA

E.O.S.

SAMARIA GORGE

NEW AGIA ROUMELI

LEFKA ORI
Walk 3

OMALOS

XYLOSKALON

GINGILOS

- Strong walking shoes or boots (ankle support and a steel shanked sole are most advisable).
- Sunglasses, sunscreen and a hat.
- Warm sweater, nylon jacket and long pants.
- Camping gear.
- Compass, knife, whistle and flashlight.
- Adequate food and water. (There is fresh water at the midpoint
- Katsivelli.)
- First aid kit.

* Please inform someone of your location and expected date of return.

* Do not attempt this hike alone.

Due to the dramatic rise and fall of the landscape on this hike, it is an advantage to begin at 1100 metres, from the mountain hamlet of Omalos (rooms to let and a couple of tavernas). Upon our arrival in the late afternoon, we set off for the E.O.S. (Greek Mountaineering Club) Kallergi Hut (1680 m) only 1½ hours away. Overlooking the Samaria Gorge from a spectacular perch, the stone hut is a perfect destination for the evening. Some information about the Kallergi Hut:

- open from May 1 – Oct. 20 each year;
- beds for 50 people;
- dinner and breakfast are served;
- reservations can be made in advance, but no one is turned away;
- inexpensive with still lower rates for International Mountain Club members;
- can be opened in winter for those interested in cross country skiing;
- Hania telephone 0821-30821, 20030.

Follow the paved road south from Omalos for 30 minutes (3 kms) before making a left turn at a blue and white E.O.S. sign onto a dirt road. Stay on the rough road for the 1 hour climb to the Kallergi Hut. (Option: there is a steep shortcut at the second switchback along the dirt road.) (1½h).

The next morning rise early with high expectations for walking in the highest mountain range on Crete. On the way out from the hut, stop at the outhouse that hangs precariously over the side of the gorge. If heights frighten you, the view through the toilet seat will appear like a nightmare. Turn right onto the dirt road that leads up to the hut and continue in a northeast direction for about 1½ hours before reaching the trailhead. (We were fortunate to get a ride in the back of a shepherd's truck for this section of road. The walking time is estimated in the strongest sense of the word.) (3h).

The trailhead is not obvious, but with the following information it should be accessible. The dirt road follows along behind a steep ridge that separates it from the Samaria Gorge. The road emerges from behind the ridge at a rather sharp switchback, with closeup views into the gorge and back up to the Kallergi Hut. The road continues downhill in a sweeping arc, with many bee hives and cement reservoir discernable below. At the switchback, however, the trail begins – leading away from the outside of the bend amongst an unlikely field of ferns. Only 5 metres after leaving the dirt road, red waymarkings (both arrows and dots) lead the way. The rough trail ploughs quickly up the side of the wall of mountain, soon to become Melindaou. Follow the markings carefully to the top of the ridge. The trail then follows in a northerly direction (a left turn) to the top of peak 1. From the trailhead it takes 1 hour to reach this point. (4h).

Once atop peak 1 it is not difficult to plot the trail between the peaks along the ridge. The ridge leads easterly, eventually peaking at the lofty summit of Melindaou (2133 m). Peak 1 is a good vantage point from which to orient yourself (break out the compass) before continuing. Form a mental picture of the shapes and locations of the surrounding landforms to accompany the map. Among the grey limestone peaks, Samaria Gorge appears lush and green – the view deep inside is breathtaking!

From Peak 1, walk downhill a short distance before ascending to Peak 2 on the trail just to the left (northwest) of the ridge. Follow the infrequent red waymarkings, reaching the small summit in only ½ hour. The view from the top is far reaching on a clear day. During our June visit, the two outstretched arms protruding into the Mediterranean from the northwest corner were in sharp focus. Our panorama continued counterclockwise around the far west end of the island, to the craggy south coast cliffs that plummet into the Libyan Sea. (4½h).

After Peak 2, continue along the ridge that forms an arbitrary boundary for the wide opening of Samaria. In just 20 minutes the trail passes to the south side of Peak 3. Follow the occasional red markings for another 10 minutes to a merging of trails in a hollow after Peak 3. Continue in an easterly direction guided by bright splashes of yellow paint. (5h).

It is 50 minutes from the beginning of the more frequent yellow waymarkings to the peak of Melindaou. The trail rises along the ridge towards Melindaou, but passes below the summit on the southern side. There seems to be an over abundance of possible trails in this area. If you lose the yellow markings, head for the summit of Melindaou to get your bearings. (5h 50m).

As our small group was approaching Melindaou, we were startled by an incredibly low overflight of a full grown eagle. We watched in near paralysis as the large bird of prey circled upwards on warm air from the sea, until disappearing over a crest.

At the summit of Melindaou, enjoy the fabulous views: Hania to the north; Samaria, for the last time, to the south; and the broad face of Pachnes (2452 m) to the southeast. In the foreground is the wide valley floor on which the trail will emerge far below. From the top, either backtrack to the point you left the trail, or catch the yellow dashes on a lower ridge to the southeast of Melindaou. (Do not take the ridge running nearly due east from the summit as it lies to the left of the correct trail.) The trail soon leads into a gully between the two aforementioned ridges. Follow the well marked trail, but beware of a swallow hole cave located near the trail just before the valley floor.

After hiking across scree for much of the day, the smooth dirt path along the valley floor feels like carpet to weary feet. Soon, the trail leads past a thistle shrouded well (50 minutes from the summit). The water is very bad and should only be used with water purification tablets. There are places to camp along the wide valley, but the best areas (with much better water) are an hour further on. (6h 40m).

Pass a tiny stone shelter built leaning into a large boulder in 10 minutes. Follow the trail just to the right, until reaching an adjoining valley. Look back to 2 mitata (stone shepherds' huts No. 1) as you turn right before a wall of mountains. Pass to the right and continue around the base of Papa Balomata (2125 m).

The trail begins to take on a well worn appearance as you enter the isolated world of the Sfakion shepherds. Pass another large mitato (No. 2) in 15 minutes and follow the good trail due east from there. Pass into the barren mountains with Pachnes ahead in full view. Continue east, passing near the foot of Pachnes and the mountains that flank it. It is ½ hour from the stone hut (No. 2) to the shepherds' enclave of Katsiveli (hut No. 3). There is good water here and places to camp nearby. (we found a flat and protected depression about 5 minutes before reaching Katsiveli.) Please ask the shepherds' permission for camping and water if they are within sight. A little miming with the word "endaxi?" (okay?) will usually suffice. (7½h).

It wasn't until this point in the hike that we met another living soul. As the sun was fading behind the Lefka Ori, a lone shepherd toting a rifle happened by our encampment. We talked for a while over brandy about the beauty of the area and the ascent to Pachnes. He then loped off over the hills with an ease and quickness befitting a professional athlete. We stayed up a little longer to watch the full moon rise over Pachnes, and soon began to doubt the reality of cities and towns.

******

Optional: Ascent of Pachnes:
There are two possible ascents to the second highest peak on the island. In the centre of Crete, Psiloritis (2456 m) stands a scant 4 metres taller than Pachnes. The summit can be taken from the north (leaving Katsiveli) or from the ridge to the east. There is no trail during the 1½ hour climb – from either direction – to the top. It is a good idea to leave your packs below during the 3 hour hike up and back. Examine the route on the map if the climb to the top is enticing.

*****

We were glad to have warm bags and a tent for the cool, clear night. Awakening early the next morning we walked the short distance to Katsiveli to freshen up at the well. A shepherd there called us over for a glass of fresh (very!) milk to help us on our way. At his trash-strewn abode, Georgos' gruff friendliness was soon interrupted by the sudden report of a rifle. He casually explained that his brother was hunting partridge just over the hill.

It was time to leave the summer pastures of the Lefka Ori behind, before the heat of the day arrived. The trail from Katsiveli is marked and abundantly clear as it passes around the conical peak of Modaki (2224 m). The sparse vegetation begins to thin out to almost nothing in the cratered limestone environment. A few petrified rocks and chunks of crystallized quartz are scattered among the rocky rubble. The trail continues its roller coaster incline to another stone hut (No. 4) with fairly good water in 1 hour 20 minutes.

After hut No. 4, the trail becomes solid stone as it traverses along the side of a threatening black cauldron. This awesome landscape evokes feelings of repulsion, though it is somehow beautiful. Little blotches of intensely coloured alpine flowers manage to survive in the desert-like setting. Be careful of the inverted cone opening of a large cave that is dangerously close to the trail - 40 minutes from hut No. 4. It is 1½ hours between shepherds' huts No. 4 and No. 5 (9h).

From hut No. 5, the trail occasionally becomes rough cobblestone, tracking through an ever changing lunerscape. The trail descends quickly for 40 minutes before emerging at a reddish dirt road. Follow the switchbacks of the main road downhill (the shortcuts are often more time consuming) towards Anopoli, 3 hours away. The road is a welcome change for the feet and it allows for glorious views to the sea. It passes through a thin pine forest alive with the sounds of nature. (10½h).

Arriving at Anopoli (rooms to let, taverna, kafeneion), with a new eye for greenery, is a homecoming of sorts. The old man at the kafeneion will question you endlessly about your odyssey through the Lefka Ori. Stop and enjoy the company of others under a shade tree, before plotting your next move. Looking back to the lofty peaks from a comfortable chair, there is a sense of satisfaction, almost inner strength, in knowing what lies beyond. (14h).

The small coastal village of Loutro was the ideal place for us to spend a few days after the long hike. It is tastefully situated around a small harbour with several tavernas at the outermost perimeter. It is accessible only by boat or foot due to the surrounding wall of rock. Anopoli is connected by a good footpath that descends to Loutro, 1 hour away. From the first kafeneion, pass by the statue and follow the asphalt road in a southeast direction through town. A small dirt road tracks to the right just before the sign "Leaving Anopoli". Take this road past a couple of whitewashed houses before turning right again on the footpath. The path zig-zags down the ridge to Loutro visible in the distance. (for more information on this area, see walk 7.) (15h).

4) GINGILOS SUMMIT

Walking Time: 5 hours.

Access: Follow the coastal road from Hania in a westerly direction. In 2 kms. turn left (south) onto a smaller road towards Lakki (25 kms.) and on to the Omalos Plain (37kms.). The walk begins at the southern edge of the plain at a point called Xyloskalon.

Bus Journey Time: 1¼ hours.
There are 4 buses daily from Hania to Xyloskalon during the summer months. (Ask for the bus to the Samaria Gorge – it is the same starting point.) The same number of buses make the return trip.

Description: When people arrive at Xyloskalon at the top of the Samaria Gorge, they invariably comment about the imposing rock face of Gingilos Peak (2080 m). The craggy limestone mountain

TIME AND TOPOGRAPHY

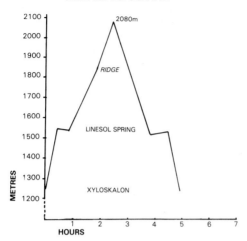

appears due south of the wooden steps that mark the entrance to the popular gorge (see walk 5). The sheer northern face of Gingilos drops off into the chasm below, providing plenty of fodder for visitors' cameras. Making the trip to the top is unthinkable at first glance, but a walking trail comes discreetly around the back of the peak, revealing the summit to those of us with no urge to use ropes and karabiners. Though the hike is decidedly rewarding it is not altogether easy, especially close to the windblown summit.

At Xyloskalon there are snacks and beverages that may be purchased before setting out. It will feel a bit odd to be among the ebullient preparations of those walking the gorge, and then heading in the opposite direction. The trail begins at a bright yellow sign posted just to the back of the lodge. (This "tourist pavilion" has a taverna and a few rooms to let. As the rooms fill up early it is better to reserve in advance.) Although the trail has no waymarkings it is obvious as it rises quickly uphill.

During the first 45 minutes, the loose rubble trail ascends westerly along a ridge, offering ever widening views of the Omalos Plain. After this quick rise there is a gentle drop in the midst of sparse trees and natural rock sculptures. This lasts for 30 minutes as the good path leads through a rock archway and on to the ice cold spring of Linesol. The respite from the steep grade ends here, fill up your water bottles and ready yourself for the last half of the hike upwards. (45m).

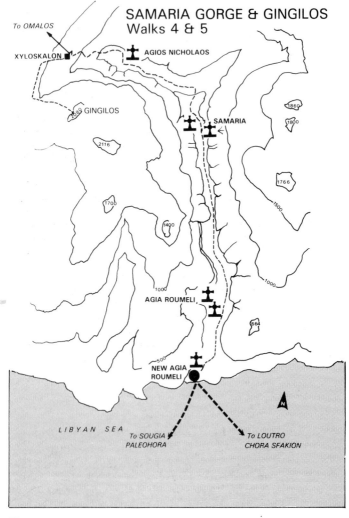

SAMARIA GORGE & GINGILOS
Walks 4 & 5

To OMALOS

XYLOSKALON

AGIOS NICHOLAOS

GINGILOS

SAMARIA

AGIA ROUMELI

NEW AGIA ROUMELI

LIBYAN SEA

To SOUGIA PALEOHORA

To LOUTRO CHORA SFAKION

N

For the next 45 minutes, the visible but scree covered trail leads to the left of a broad rock slide. The path switches back frequently during the rather steep climb. Emerging at a ridge with soaring views to the sea is an accomplishment, but the summit is still ½ hour away. The cold air at this altitude will likely bring on a few unexpected shivers. It is a good point to be on the watch for large birds of prey. We spotted a booted eagle during our mid-July visit. Another possible sight is that of the Cretan wild goat (also called "Kri-Kri"), as this area is its last natural habitat. With busloads of people walking down the gorge, the agile goats are occasionally spotted along the upper reaches. Keep a lookout for their distinctive spread of horns. (2h).

The last ½ hour of the hike is marked with red waymarkings; a large arrow points the way up from the ridge. Stay with the red paint or rock piles because the area near the summit is dangerous: deep swallow holes and sudden precipices. The final ascent requires the use of both hands and feet in some places. The views down can be staggering especially if vertigo is a problem for you. The summit is actually mild in comparison with getting there, but the views are fabulous on a clear day. Contribute a stone to the large pile marking the top of the round cone and enjoy the 360 degree panorama: drop into Samaria Gorge; across to the even higher summits of the Lefka Ori (see walk 3); closeup views of the Omalos Plain; the promontory of Akrotiri and Hania; around the west end of Crete and finally plunging into the sea from the south coast cliffs. (2½h).

Of course, the return trip is much like the walk up, except that the view into Samaria comes more naturally. The scree on the trail prevents a rapid descent, as the footing requires slow and sure attention to the bottom. Once down to the lodge, take a seat on the balcony looking out toward Gingilos. It is the ideal place to reflect on having conquered the lofty peak – if only for a moment. (5h).

5) SAMARIA GORGE

The park is officially open May 1 – October 31.

Walking Time: 5 hours from Xyloskalon.

Access: Follow the coastal road in a westerly direction from Hania. In 2 kms. turn left (south) onto a smaller road towards Lakki and on to the Omalos Plain. It is another 5 kms. to the southern edge of the plain at Xyloskalon (Wooden Steps) where the gorge

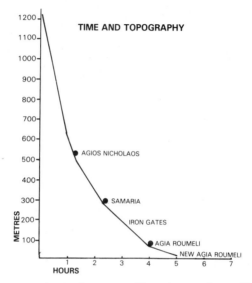

TIME AND TOPOGRAPHY

METRES

HOURS

AGIOS NICHOLAOS

SAMARIA

IRON GATES

AGIA ROUMELI

NEW AGIA ROUMELI

begins in earnest. There is a tourist pavilion with a cafeteria and a small number of beds (reservations recommended) at this point. If you drive to Xyloskalon it is a long return trip to retrieve the car.

Bus Journey Time: 1½ hours.

There are 4 buses daily from Hania to the beginning of the gorge at Xyloskalon during summer. In the off-season other arrangements must be made.

Return:

From the bottom of the gorge there are several alternatives. From New Agia Roumeli it is possible to take a small boat east to Loutro (See walks 7 and 8) and on to Chora Sfakion. In summer, boats leave 5 times daily and there is a connecting bus line from Chora Sfakion to Hania. There is also a beautiful, albeit long, hike to the same destination along a small marked footpath (See walk 6). A boat leaves every evening to the west stopping in Sougia (See walk 11) and then on to Paleohora. Of

The Dragon Arum flourishes in springtime within the shaded confines of the Samaria Gorge.

course, you may hike back along the same route which takes about 7 hours.

Description: The Samaria Gorge fulfils even the most inflated expectations. The strenuous hike captures the stunning natural beauty of the 18km. cleft and the surrounding peaks of the Lefka Ori (White Mountains). Thousands of visitors trek through Samaria each year, but it is a place that can absorb the throngs without losing its appeal. Once to the bottom, the feeling of accomplishment is pervasive and swimming in the Libyan Sea, or sipping a beer was never quite this good. But first . . .

It is perhaps best to plunge over the lip of the gorge during the coolness of early morning, accompanied by a sturdy set of walking shoes and the endurance for a 5 hour hike to the bottom. From an altitude of about 1200 metres the trail zig-zags downhill quickly. The view due east is to the second highest peak on Crete, Pachnes (2452 m). The highest, Psiloritis, located in the centre of the island is only a scant 4 metres higher. The trail is well maintained to the point of having handrails and litter bins during the rapid descent of the first hour. Then the sharp drop mellows as the trail follows the stream bed for the remainder of the way. There are 5 fresh water springs spread out along the trail to quench any thirst and grant a reprieve from the heat

In just over an hour after setting out the stone shingled chapel of Agios Nicholaos comes into view. The terraced view is accented by several towering cypress trees that are hundreds of years old. (1h 15m).

From the chapel of Agios Nicholaos it is another hour to the hamlet of Samaria. Once the stronghold of the Viglis family, Samaria is now in ruins. Along with the park attendants' quarters (telephone, first aid and running water), all that remains standing are 3 small chapels. The oldest, Ossia Maria was built in 1379 by the Venetians who were once attracted to the vast timberland in the area[1]. Both the gorge and the town derived their name from this small chapel. The name Ossia Maria was gradually shortened to Sia Maria, and finally to Samaria.

Soon after Samaria (the approximate mid-point), the gorge begins to narrow. The vegetation becomes noticeably thicker and the smells of sage, thyme and various other spices are penetrating. There are splashes of colour from several types of wildflowers, including wild orchids and irises. The gorge is also a unique habitat for the animal world. Notably, it is the natural home of the Cretan wild goat (called Agrimi, or affectionately, Kri Kri). The casual visitor is unlikely to spot one of these agile creatures, though they still abound in the area. A more likely sight would be the graceful overflight of one of the many species of eagles, falcons and vultures. Keep one eye trained for the wonders of the gorge's true inhabitants and the other carefully locked onto the rocky path.

The opposite sides of the deep canyon now loom high above in proof of the cutting force of water through stone. During the winter rains and the early spring thaw, the gorge can become an impassable

---

1. The entire island was once renowned for the wealth of timber in its thick forests. This is in direct contrast to the now pervasive rockiness. This resource was quickly depleted by the Venetians (1204 – 1669) to build galleons to support future conquests. The deforestation continued unabated under Turkish rule (1669 – 1898). Today much of the island is affected by severe soil erosion and due to the depletion of forests there is a lack of moisture during the summer months. Reforestation efforts are usually rendered impotant by the seedling hungry domestic goat.

stream. Therefore, it is recommended that the park's opening from May through October be taken with more than a shrug. While it is not difficult to imagine this torrent, in summer the water sometimes bubbles forth only to slip out of sight unexpectedly.

The narrowest point of Samaria, Called the Iron Gates, is somehow the climax of the many rewards during the long hike. Two massive stone walls face each other at a distance of only 3 metres. The effect is overwhelming, as if nature had decided at the last minute to leave enough room to pass. There is no path here, only a few carefully spaced stones to allow the hiker the dignity of dry feet. (3h).

Proceed to the small village of Old Agia Roumeli which today is nearly deserted. Most of the inhabitants moved 2 kms. to the coastal settlement of New Agia Roumeli in the late 1950s, after a major flood. The new town is located just aside from the wide stream bed close to the same site as the ancient city-state of Tarra (5th century B.C. – 5th century A.D.). Tarra was important enough to have its own coinage and there have been many other Roman and Hellenic finds in the area. (See the Archaeological Museum in Hania.) The imposing castle just behind New Agia Roumeli is said to be from the Venetian era. (4h).

New Agia Roumeli is a quiet Sfakion town that provides basic services (tavernas, rooms to let and boat transportation) to weary hikers. There is also a clean, rocky beach beckoning those wanting to enjoy a cool swim.

6) NEW AGIA ROUMELI – ARADENA – ANOPOLI

Walking Time: 6¾ hours.

Access: This is a connecting route from the bottom of the Samaria Gorge (See walk 5) at New Agia Roumeli.

The area is also accessible by frequent boat service (summer only) from the south coast villages of Paleohora, Sougia, Loutro and Chora Sfakion.

Return: From Anopoli to Chora Sfakion there is one early morning bus. An expensive "local taxi" may also be arranged just by asking around. There is bus service 4 times daily from Chora Sfakion to Hania.

Only 1 hour away on the south coast is the village of Loutro (See page 69 for directions). There is boat service from Loutro to Chora Sfakion 3–4 times daily in summer. See walk 8 for a beautiful 2 hour

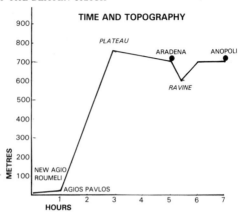

TIME AND TOPOGRAPHY

walk to Chora Sfakion.

Description: This is simply a connecting route for those people that didn't feel that the Samaria Gorge was enough of a challenge. Rather than taking a boat from Agia Roumeli to Chora Sfakion, it is quite possible to achieve the same end on a marked, overland route. It is a long and strenuous hike that covers some of the island's most scenic and isolated terrain. With an early morning start, this walk can be completed comfortably in a day. Just be certain to carry along enough liquids and food for the entire journey, because there are none to be found along the way.

A long, rocky beach extends to the west of Agia Roumeli, Keep your first hour's course on a lone trail by the beach, past several fine coves, to the chapel of Agios Pavlos (Saint Paul). From afar the chapel is hardly distinguishable, but the red tiled roof soon becomes clear against the backdrop of the Libyan Sea. It is said that when Paul was taken to Rome, he came ashore and baptized many pagans at a nearby spring. At the small chapel, a trail leads sharply up the hillside before splitting in 15 min. Take the left fork up the steep grade into a pine forest. (The right fork leads to Loutro along a difficult coastal route.) Traverse several rock slides during the ascent on a visible and winding footpath. Just before reaching the lip of the plateau, an immaculate cobblestone track leads the way. It is 2 hours of uphill walking from Agios Pavlos to the plateau. (3h).

On top is a red clay trail that is rock strewn and occasionally waymarked with splotches of red paint. From this mid-point, it is 2

Right: A look skywards to the rocky face of Gingelos from the top rim of
Samaria. (Walk 4)

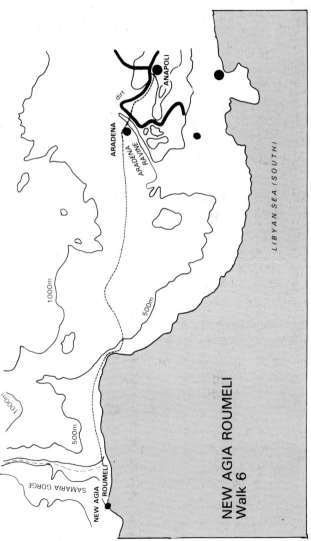

Left: During the hike down The Samaria Gorge you will be greeted by towering stone walls called the 'Iron Gates'. A steady trickle of water flows through the narrow gap. (Walk 5)

65

Rocky beach to the east of New Agia Roumeli.

hours to the hamlet of Aradena. The path crosses a shepherd's encampment and shortly thereafter, a red arrow indicates an important right turn in an easterly direction. (If you continue too far up the trail, the deserted Monastery of Agios Ioannis and a small village of the same name will eventually block your way.) Follow through the trees until joining a road that, in time, leads between stone walls in the midst of untended olive groves. The straggling village of Aradena, with its few remaining residents, is now a pot-pourri of crumbling stonework. Built on the protective edge of the Aradena Ravine, the once thriving village derived its name from the nearby ancient site of Aradin. (5h).

Beginning near a whitewashed chapel, a winding cobblestone supply route descends quickly into the depths of the ravine and right back up the other side. A bridge is under construction, but until it is completed, this hour-long route to the opposite side must be taken. (A walk through the Aradena Ravine to Livandiana, is nearly impossible without experience and equipment.) The rugged terrain of the Aradena Ravine brings to mind an article written by Charles Edwards, published in *The Nineteenth Century* periodical. He writes of the warring relationship between the Turkish Moslems and the

Sfakion people during the latter years of Turkish rule: "They dislike the snow as they dislike the steady aim of the Sfakiots, and the dreadful snares which nature herself has contrived for them among the White Mountains". The footpath on the far side of the ravine crosses the road leading to Anopoli and soon after, evolves into a raised cobblestone variety. In 30 min., merge onto a dirt road on the outskirts of the flourishing village. Pass by the chapel and cemetery on a tree-lined road, to the centre of Anopoli (taverna, rooms). (6h 45m).

7) LOUTRO LOOP

Walking Time: 6½ hours.
  4½ hours if you don't cross the Aradena Ravine.

Access: From Hania, follow the coastal road east for 32 km. until reaching a small sign indicating a right turn to Vrises. (From Rethymnon, follow the coastal road west for 39 km.). Pass through Vrises and head due south on the twisting road leading to Chora Sfakion. Continue past the villages of Askifou (51 km.) and Imbros (57 km.) (see Walk 9) until reaching the coastal settlement of Chora Sfakion (73 km).

  Bus Journey Time: 2 hours.
  There is bus service from Hania to Chora Sfakion 4 times daily. (From Rethymnon, take a bus to Vrises along the Rethymnon/Hania bus route – every ½ hour. Change buses in Vrises to reach Chora Sfakion – 4 times daily.)

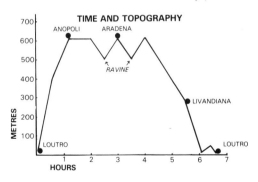

67

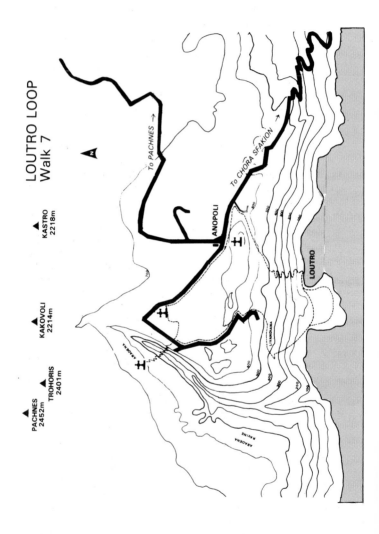

From Chora Sfakion there is a boat 4 times daily to Loutro or take a beautiful 2 hour walk (see walk 8) along the coast.

Description: This is a walk for those of you lucky enough to have found Loutro. The walk begins and ends at this jewel of a town on the south coast. Though the trail rises and drops rather dramatically during this 6½ hour walk, (save 2 hours by not crossing the Aradena Ravine) the rewards are plenty. Along the way there are beautiful views to the south coast, several Sfakion villages and the narrow ravine of Aradena to look forward to.

Loutro is the kind of place that could lull you into believing there are no problems in the world. The setting is harmonious and it is a blessing to be away from the noise and exhaust of automobiles. The 14 summer inhabitants (5 in winter) operate a few tavernas and rent modern rooms to the smattering of travellers that happen on the village.

A well maintained path visibly leads up the steep mountain side behind Loutro. Find the trailhead at the east end of town just behind the 2 storey whitewashed buildings along the waterfront. The frequent switchbacks of the trail straighten out shortly before coming to the top of the ridge in 1¼ hours, at the upland plain of Anopoli. Turn left onto a dirt road as the trail ends, and left again onto the asphalt road that leads to the main cluster of houses. (1h 15m).

The town of Anopoli (tavernas, rooms) is nestled along the broad plain with the immense massif of Lefka Ori just to the north, and a steep ridge on the sea side. It is this rugged environment, combined with the sturdy character of the Sfakion people that produced folk heroes. One former resident of Anopoli was Daskaloyannis (John the Teacher), a wealthy merchant who led an ill-fated uprising against the Turks in 1770. Even though the region of Sfakia enjoyed many freedoms under Turkish rule, it was not enough for this native son of Crete. For his part in the rebellion, Daskaloyannis was flogged to death on the Pasha's orders and Sfakia was shown no mercy.

The asphalt road that leads through Anopoli splits in 10 minutes at a kafeneion; take the left fork towards Aradena. Inside the kafeneion is a fascinating diagram of a 2 km. long cave in the area that was explored by a British spelunking club. Follow along the dirt road for 5 minutes to reach another split, next to a chapel with a cemetery. Stay to the left of the cemetery and follow under a row of trees with red waymarkings (and KKE graffiti). Just a couple of minutes after the cemetery a large red arrow will direct you left onto a footpath by a

69

The whitewashed village of Loutro on the south coast.

small group of buildings. The footpath soon becomes rough cobblestone, leading to the Aradena Ravine in 30 minutes. Cross the main dirt road and soon afterwards you will be looking at a staggering accomplishment: the winding cobblestone path that leads down into the Aradena Ravine and right back up the other side. (2h).

With the intriguing village of Aradena situated on the other side, and a tempting trail below, the decision to cross is yours. (A bridge was under construction during our visits, but a long way from finished.) It takes about 1 hour to reach the other side via the trail, even though Aradena is only a stone's throw away. Today the crumbling village boasts only 10 inhabitants, most of whom are quite old. It flourished until fairly recently, when a series of vendettas scared almost the entire population away. (3h).

A walk through the Aradena Ravine, towards Livandiana, is impossible without equipment and experience. We tried to pass through the ravine, due to conflicting information, only to be greeted by sheer 10 metre drops. Although the interior is enticing, you can still get a tempestuous feeling from the trail. (Return 4h).

Back on the east side of the ravine, there is a rough dirt road that follows downhill, away from Anopoli. Walk down the gradual slope of the dirt road through the thorny and rocky surroundings. After 45

70

minutes, the road makes a wide curve and you'll have the first views down to Livandiana. There is a visible trail, with an inconspicuous beginning, that leads there. This marked footpath follows a steeper pitch to the village of Livandiana in 45 minutes. (5½h).

The shepherds have found a good use for the thorny brunet that flourishes in this area. They place the spiny plants atop their rock walled animal pens like barbed wire. On the way into Livandiana, the trail passes one of these pens; just follow along the stone wall to the opposite side. From this point there is a good view back to the sea side opening of the Aradena Ravine.

Enjoy the mountainside setting and coastal views of Livandiana. There is flowing spring water near the top of this quiet village. As you pass through town on a stepped pathway, observe the construction and design of some of the vacant kamarospita (houses with interior archways). The long archway separates the house into functional living spaces and reduces the span of the flat roof. This design was necessary due to the lack of wood in the area. There are niches in the walls for household items and a water jug. The site of Livandiana is naturally fortified and built to insure security and defences from years of struggle. (6h).

The pathway through Livandiana continues downhill to a beach (taverna, rooms). Just 15 minutes west, at the terminus of the Aradena Ravine, is a Phoenix Beach. Its half submerged caves provide a setting for mystical exploration. After a swim, follow a well worn path back to Loutro rejoining your trail at the taverna. Ten minutes later, the red waymarkings lead to the remnants of a Venetian castle – turned goat pen. Keep to the left, it is another 10 minutes back to the welcoming ambience of Loutro. (6½h).

8) CHORA SFAKION – SWEETWATER BEACH – LOUTRO

THE SFAKIOT VERSION OF THE CREATION: The story opens with an account of all the gifts God had given to other parts of Crete – olives to Ierapetra, Ayios Vasilios and Selinou; wine to Malevesi and Kissamou; cherries to Mylopotamos and Amari. But when God got to Sfakia only rocks were left. So the Sfakiots appeared before Him armed to the teeth. "And us, Lord, how are we going to live on these rocks?" and the Almighty, looking at them with sympathy, replied in their own dialect (naturally): "Haven't you got a scrap of brains in

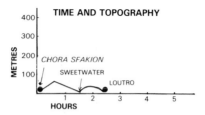

your heads? Don't you see that the lowlanders are cultivating all these riches for you?"

From Adam Hopkins' fine book entitled, *Crete, Its Past, Present and People.*

* * * * * *

Walking Time: 2¼ hours.

Access: From Hania, follow the coastal road east for 32 km. until reaching a small sign indicating a right turn to Vrises. (From Rethymnon, follow the coastal road west for 32 km.). Pass through Vrises and head due south on the twisting road leading to Chora Sfakion. Continue past the villages of Askifou (51 km.) and Imbros (57 km.) (see Walk No. 9) until reaching the coastal settlement of Chora Sfakion (73 km.).

Bus Journey Time: 2 hours.
There is bus service from Hania to Chora Sfakion 4 times daily. (From Rethymnon, take a bus to Vrises along the Rethymnon/Hania bus route – every ½ hour. Change buses in Vrises to reach Chora Sfakion – 4 times daily.)

Boat Journey Time: 20 minutes.
From Chora Sfakion there is a boat 4 times daily to and from Loutro.

Description: There is an aura of myth that has become intertwined with the history of the Sfakion region. Though it has calmed down considerably since the days of piracy and brigandage, the Sfakiots are still a rugged and proud people. This short walk begins at the centre of the Sfakion province and leads along the scraggy coast to the west. There is a good trail for much of the way, though rough in places. A fine stony beach at the mid-point, with small fresh water pools,

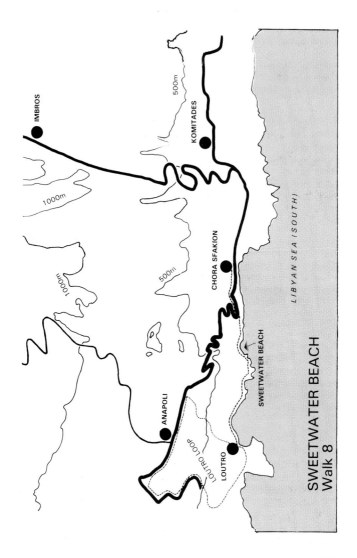

IMBROS

500m

KOMITADES

1000m

500m

CHORA SFAKION

LIBYAN SEA (SOUTH)

1000m

SWEETWATER BEACH

ANAPOLI

LOUTRO LOOP

LOUTRO

SWEETWATER BEACH
Walk 8

provides the perfect intermission. After a swim, the walk resumes towards the jewel of the south coast – Loutro.

During the 16th century, Chora Sfakion was a bustling commercial centre with a population of 3000 and a merchant fleet of 40 vessels. Once the largest town on the entire south coast; today it is only a fraction of its former self. There is a pleasant feeling gained from the steep hillside setting of the town's whitewashed houses. The sleepy port ushers in boatloads of weary hikers coming back from a long day in the Samaria Gorge (see Walk 5).

The influx of people into Sfakia has doubtlessly changed much of the uninhibited lawlessness of past centuries. There is, however, a certain preservation of tradition and superstition that holds over from the past, regardless of the law. At weddings and baptisms this is stridently expressed in the prevalence of firearms that rattle off into the night. While not obvious to the outsider, the rustling of neighbouring flocks of sheep and blood vendettas are still a way of life. On a lighter tack, is the ongoing (though rapidly diminishing) belief that passing soap from hand to hand will wash away the bonds of friendship. Certainly it is an area where passions run thick and the vitality of the people is obvious – but definitely not dangerous to foreigners, as some people steadfastly maintain.

From the bus stop, walk away from the beachfront for 100 metres before turning left onto the asphalt road leading towards Anopoli. Take the road gradually uphill in a westerly direction for 30 minutes, until the first sharp switchback. An unobtrusive trail continues along the coast from just behind the guardrail. Be careful not to follow the snaking asphalt road away from the coast – or you've gone too far. The footpath makes a slow descent and is easily visible for the entire walk. It leads over cobblestones and under rock ledges while inviting resplendent views to the sea. As the trail nears sea-level, you are forced to cross over a couple of old rock slides. The path is waymarked and none too difficult. Just 50 minutes from the trailhead the small stones of Sweetwater Beach come under your feet. (1½h).

The cliff enclosed beach is accessible only on foot or by the occasional fisherman's caique that shuttles by. Fresh water lies just beneath the beach; in several places there are small pools from which to wash the seawater off. It is a beautiful place to pass a few hours before continuing on your way.

At the west end of the beach, next to the remains of a small chapel, a narrow dirt trail leads up the bluff. It is rather steep for about 5 minutes, but soon begins to level out. Carry on past the ever-present whitewashed chapel towards now visible Loutro, only 45 minutes away. (2h 15m).

The trail leads into the tiny port village from behind. Loutro's charms are not immediately evident, but just sit for a short while at the quiet waterfront and let the slow lifestyle of the place take hold. Enveloped by the surmounting mountains of the Lefka Ori, there is a content feeling from the tranquil environment. A few tavernas are situated along the water's edge and there are modern rooms to let. If your curiosity has been raised by the eye-catching trail etched in the cliffs behind, take a look at the Loutro Loop (Walk 7). This walk explores some of the nearby villages while covering dramatic terrain. To the west, at the end of the Aradena Ravine is Phoenix Beach (named after the ancient port of Phoenice) with its several half submerged caves. Why not stay for a few days? or longer . . .

9)   IMBROS RAVINE

Walking Time:	2 hours 20 minutes.
Access:	From Hania, follow the coastal road east for 32 km. until reaching a small sign indicating a right turn to Vrises. (From Rethymnon, follow the coastal road west for 39 km.). Pass through the tree lined streets of Vrises and head due south on the road leading to Chora Sfakion. Continue past the plain of Askifou (51 km.) and stop at the village of Imbros (57 km.). It is quite possible to take a bus from the end of the walk to retrieve a car left in Imbros.

Bus Journey Time: 1¼ hours.
There is bus service from Hania to Chora Sfakion 4 times daily. (From Rethymnon, take a bus to Vrises along the Rethymnon/Hania bus route – every ½ hour. Change buses in Vrises to reach Imbros – 4 times daily). The walk begins at the village of Imbros just 13 km. before Chora Sfakion.

The walk ends at the village of Komitades. Continue west on the asphalt road through town for 15 minutes to connect with the main bus route (Chora Sfakion – Hania/Rethymnon). Be sure to have a current time table to avoid a long wait on the side of the road.

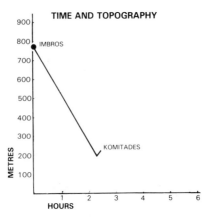

Description: Only 16 km. east of the Samaria Gorge (see Walk 5) is the nearly unknown Imbros Ravine. It descends to the south coast in a roughly parallel manner as Samaria, and is considered one of the 5 great ravines that come sweeping down to sea level from the White Mountains. The trail, once an old supply route, drops gently into the untamed setting. There is food and water at both ends of the relatively easy walk, and the trail is wide enough to alleviate worries of scratched legs for those wearing shorts. The isolated splendour of Imbros can be seen in just over 2 hours. It is a perfect alternative for those who prefer the wonders of nature in solitude.

Imbros is located at the south end of the alpine plain of Askifou in the heart of Sfakia. The waters that collected on the upland plain eventually cut through stone: draining into the Libyan Sea and creating the narrow ravine along the way. The trail begins, near a green shrine, just off the main road on the southern outskirts of Imbros. (The village consists of only a few houses, a taverna and a bakery.) Drop to the dry stream bed and follow the well worn path into the mouth of the ravine. From time to time the trail lapses into cobblestones recalling the history of the area.

Until around 1960 there wasn't a good road connecting Chora Sfakion with the plain of Askifou. The best overland route required the end to end completion of the Imbros Ravine. An older gentleman from Chora Sfakion recalled the trip, made with heavy sacks of flour, with a mixture of pain and nostalgia. Today, a twisting asphalt road passes high above the deep ravine offering superficial views of the beauty that lies below.

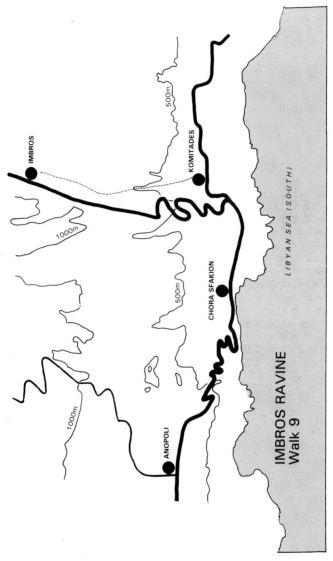

IMBROS
KOMITADES
500m
1000m
500m
CHORA SFAKION
1000m
ANOPOLI
LIBYAN SEA (SOUTH)

IMBROS RAVINE
Walk 9

Sfakia – the region – was the only area of Crete never to be completely subjugated under Turkish rule. No doubt this was due to two important factors: inaccessible terrain and the unconforming character of the people. Despite their relative autonomy, many revolts and rebellions against the Turks were spearheaded from this outpost. Even today, the inhabitants of Sfakia consider themselves above the law. There is a love of arms in this region: sheep stealing and the resultant vendettas are still a way of life.

The trail doesn't require much description because it simply follows the dry stream bed. Above, there are many pine trees growing from the grassy slopes. But, soon the sides of the ravine fold inward, and in 45 minutes there is a separation of a scant 2 metres between looming cliff walls. The feeling is almost mystical as the sandy path squeezes its way through a series of confining curves. The narrowness of this area produces a cooling effect that allows for 3 different climatic zones in a relatively short distance. It is a perfect refuge for many species of plants, including several endemic varieties. (1h).

It is 30 minutes beyond this narrowest of points to a spectacular stone archway. A thick rock face easily supports the gap – 15 metres high and 6 metres across at the bottom. (1½h).

As the stream bed widens into the plain of Imbros, the rock bluffs fade into grassy knolls and the Libyan Sea comes into view. Some 30 minutes from the archway, the trail leaves the stream bed. Before reaching an enclosing fence, turn right onto a pathway leading between stone walls. Turn right again, to the now visible town of Komitades. There are a couple of inviting tavernas in this small village. Now it's time to sit back and take stock of the beauties that passed before. (2h 20m).

10) ASKIFOU PLATEAU – FRANGOKASTELLO

Walking Time: 5 hours.

Access: From Hania, follow the coastal road east for 32 km. until reaching a small sign indicating a right turn for Vrises. (From Rethymnon, follow the coastal road west for 39 km.) Pass through the tree lined streets of Vrises and head due south on the road leading to Chora Sfakion. Continue until reaching the village of Kares, at the north end of the Askifou plain.

TIME AND TOPOGRAPHY

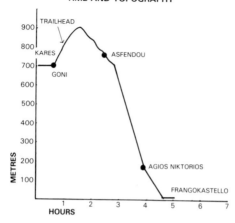

Bus Journey Time: 1 hour.

There is bus service from Hania to Chora Sfakion 4 times daily. (From Rethymnon, take a bus to Vrises along the Rethymnon/Hania bus route – every ½ hour. Change buses in Vrises and take a bus towards Chora Sfakion (4 times daily.) The walk begins 19 km. before Chora Sfakion at the town of Kares along the edge of the Askifou plain.

Return: The walk ends at Frangokastello where bus service is sporadic at best. If you want to spend the night, there is a morning bus from Frangokastello to Chora Sfakion, or 3 times a week to Plakias. There is bus service 4 times daily from Chora Sfakion to Hania/Rethymnon. Since Chora Sfakion is only 14 km. away, taking a taxi (or hitching) to the bus route is a good option.

Description: This is a walk in which to delight in some of the well hidden beauties of Crete, in an area thick with history. The trek begins in the heart of the Sfakion region at the upland plain of Askifou; passing through the hinterlands and down to the south coast. Along the way a wide cobblestone track, that once served as a supply route, mysteriously appears. The trail leads through several remote villages, and winds down a deep ravine before ending at the

79

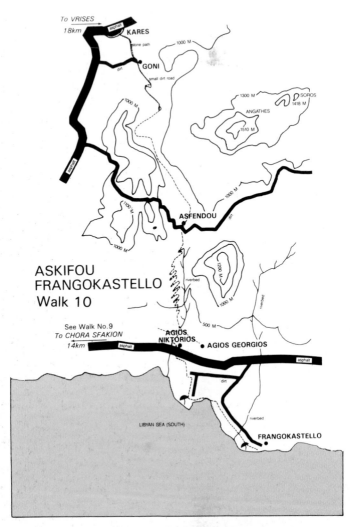

To VRISES
18km
asphalt
KARES

stone path

GONI

dirt

small dirt road

1000 M

1300 M

SOROS
1418 M

ANGATHES

1510 M

1000 M

asphalt

1000 M

1200 M

ASFENDOU

dirt

1000 M

1000 M

1200 M

ASKIFOU
FRANGOKASTELLO
Walk 10

riverbed

1000 M

riverbed

500 M

See Walk No.9
To CHORA SFAKION
14km
asphalt

AGIOS
NIKTORIOS

AGIOS GEORGIOS

asphalt

dirt

riverbed

LIBYAN SEA (SOUTH)

FRANGOKASTELLO

Right: The whitewashed village of Chora Sfakion (Walk 8)

The well-preserved fortress of Frangokastello is dwarfed by the imposing backdrop of peaks and chasms.

impressive fortress of Frangokastello. The Venetian Lion of St. Mark stands guard over a pristine, white sand beach that still remains rather undiscovered.

The Askifou plateau sits like a patchwork quilt of light yellows and greens, in the shadow of the towering peaks of the Lefka Ori. Within its narrow boundaries are a couple of misplaced hills, on which the ruins of a Turkish fortress still look out over a people that were never subdued by its presence. The form of agriculture in this isolated area has, in many respects, hardly changed since Minoan times. There are few modern implements to ease the backbreaking labour. The small size of the fields betray modern machinery and family plots continue to divide with each passing generation. There are 5 small villages that are situated along the untillable areas of the plain. The walk begins at the northernmost village of Kares in front of the bakery. It is best to begin in the coolness of early morning and to bring enough food and water for the entire trip.

A small paved road leads into Kares from the main Hania/Chora Sfakion route. Turn right in front of the bakery and pass through the tiny village to the south. In Kares, there is also a kafeneion (café) and a small market. Just on the outskirts, merge left onto a cement road, and left again onto a stone track that rambles between two fields. The road ends in a "T" at the fortress topped hill.

******

OPTION: The fortress remains are like a lure for those curious enough to scramble up the hillside. There is not much of a trail, but reaching the top allows magnificent views over the plain and to the backdrop of the Lefka Ori (White Mountains). However, the image of the fortress is better from below. The easiest route is to turn left at the "T" near the base of the hill and continue around to the opposite side. On the back side there is a fence that can serve as a rough guideline for the trail – it takes about 20 minutes to reach the top. The walk up the front side over loose rubble is considerably steeper, but still quite possible. Once to the top, there is a cobblestone path that connects both hills. A shepherd's makeshift fence is the last surmountable obstacle.

******

Turn right to the "T" and walk along the base of the hill until the road fades out. Move to a parallel track that leads between fence-topped stone walls just 10 metres above. After 10 minutes, turn left onto an asphalt road that leads to the small hillside village of Goni at the narrow southeast end of the plain. Pass to the right of Goni towards a cleft in the hills ahead. (30m).

Just outside of Goni the road reverts to dirt and in ½ hour it ends altogether. At the turnaround at the end of the dirt road, the footpath begins. Take the trail to the left, into the fold of the mountains. (A well trodden trail to the right leads only to a shepherd's hut.) Follow the occasional red dots up the gentle slope for 20 minutes before the trail splits. A red arrow shows the correct path to the left. (1h).

The sporadic red waymarkings are not much help in crossing to the other side of a field of thistle. Step gingerly to the left side of the prickly patch and in 10 minutes you will reach the other side. On the opposite side is the obvious cobblestone path that will make the rest of the going easier.

The size of the wide path, that seemingly begins out in the middle of nowhere, is staggering. Although wide enough for a car, it is obviously meant for animals or walking. The old supply route likely dates to Venetian rule, but no one we questioned was sure. Today the condition varies widely, with some sections remarkably complete and others in ill-maintained rubble. Carry on down the visible path to a pasture with 2 wells and a water trough cut from solid stone. It is 20 minutes to a similar spot with a well – the water is far from desirable at either place. (2h).

After the second watering area the small town of Asfendou comes into view. The trail is clear, but the cobblestones are frequently not to be seen. In 5 minutes there is a split, take the left fork around what appears to be the wrong side of a small mountain. Red waymarkings will reassure your choice. In another 5 minutes take a right fork, and soon the trail is accompanied by a 2 metre high stone wall. The path joins a dirt road that leads down around a curve to a kafeneion (only beverages are served). Steps lead up to a large porch, but the ill-placed sign keeps the place incognito. Chances are you will hear lively discussion emanating from the once whitewashed concrete building. (2½h).

The 80 or so Asfendou residents rely on flocks of sheep and goats for their livelihood. Until 30 years ago there wasn't an auto route connecting Asfendou with the nearby villages. Before this time, the only passage required walking the same route we take, up to Askifou or down to the south coast.

The trail resumes a short way from the front of the kafeneion, and leads down a tree-shrouded gully. Stone walls mark the sides for 15 minutes before the deep canyon begins in earnest. The beautiful area that the path covers is saturated in human toil; whether from the labours of building the stone trail, or the countless trips taken up and down its carefully placed stones. Today, it is a sage scented masterpiece of Cretan wilds, that has been virtually forgotten. Soon the enveloping nature is accented by a view to the Libyan Sea, and a bit later to the village of Agios Niktorios (Agios Georgios on most maps). It is a 1½ hour descent on the winding trail to the coastal plain. Towards the end of the ravine, bend your steps to Agios Niktorios on a marked and loose stone path. The trail becomes a dirt road just before reaching the town; continue to the asphalt and turn left. (4h).

As you walk along the asphalt, the square fortress of Frangokastel-lo comes into distant sight. Closer, and more importantly in summer, is a beautiful sandy beach – now only 20 minutes east of Agios Niktorios. There is a commemorative shrine, just as the road turns an improbable direction (away from the sea). About 15 metres before the shrine, a small path leads down, along the left side of a rock outcrop, to a dirt track. Turn left on the dirt road and continue for a couple of minutes to the fenced area of new olive trees. Turn right next to the fence and in 10 minutes you will arrive at a clean

83

refreshing beach. This section of beach is pristine with fewer people than the beach near the fortress – but if you need inspiration for a sandcastle . . . (4½h).

It is 30 minutes east along a paved road to the well preserved fortress with four corner towers. Along the way are a few tavernas and rooms to let for the night. The old fort, rooted along a sandy beach, appears dwarfed by the imposing backdrop of peaks and chasms. Perhaps it is this rugged and dominant landscape that gave the Sfakions enough courage to continue fighting against Venetian and later, Turkish rule. In 1828 a celebrated battle for independence was fought against the Turks at Frangokastello. Hundreds of Sfakions led by Hadzi Michali were killed in the hopeless fight, against far greater numbers. The locals maintain that each March in the soft light of dawn the ghosts of the soldiers reappear. The mirage is known as *drosoulites* or simply – "Dew Shadows".

11) SOUGIA – ANCIENT LISSOS – PALEOHORA

Walking Time: 1¼ hours from Sougia to Lissos (Return trip necessary) 6½ hours from Sougia to Paleohora.

Access: Sougia lies 67 kms. south of Hania on the road that leads to Alikianos (12 kms.) from the western side of the city. Continue south past Sembronas (36 kms.) on a twisting road that eventually reaches Sougia, on the south coast. A car may be a hindrance if the walk (or boat/walk combination) to Paleohora is considered.

Bus Journey Time: 2 hours.
The bus leaves Hania each afternoon and returns from Sougia early the next morning. It is a colourful bus ride as the villagers carry on their errands during the trip. (We stopped to lash on someone's newly repaired tyre, to pick up newspapers for one village and the daily bread for another.)

Each day there is a boat making the run from Sougia to Lissos to Paleohora, and the reverse. The boat runs fairly regularly in summer, but the schedule may vary with demand and weather conditions. There is also boat service (summer only) from Sougia to Agia Roumeli (see Walks 11

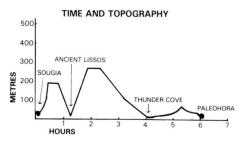

and 6), to Loutro (see Walk 7) and on to Chora
Sfakia.

Description: The village of Sougia (pronounced Souya) is situated
along one of the most attractive pieces of waterfront on the entire
southern coast. Once the site of ancient Syia, this area flourished
during the Roman and first Byzantine eras, only to be destroyed by
the Saracen Arabs (823 – 961 A.D.). Today the village is just large
enough to cover all basic needs (hotel, market, rooms and a couple
tavernas) while retaining its individual character and not succumbing
to resort status. A clean rocky beach is spread out in front of Sougia
and the view of the Lafka Ori (White Mountains) is nothing short of
spectacular. Along the wide beach are several protected coves and a
fresh-water shower.

   Follow the boardwalk in a westerly direction to the port. Just past
is the trailhead to Lissos/Paleohora. Looking at the hills rising behind
the colourful boats, the cleft that the trail follows is easily
discernable. There is a sign marking the beginning; multicoloured
dots and small piles of stones mark the rest of the way. The trail rises
quickly into a rocky ravine affording wonderful views of the coast
and the mountains beyond.

   Continue along the trail, for an hour or so, before dropping into
ancient Lissos from a ridge. From above, the once thriving
population of Lissos is easy to distinguish due to the many ruins left
behind. The city was tucked into a protected mountain valley with
only a small cove exiting to the sea. Among the olive trees are a
number of remains, the most important being those from the
Greco-Roman health centre (asklepieion). (1½h).

   The sick came to this recently rediscovered site to be cured by a
mixture of medicine and magic. The centre has been partially
restored, most impressive among the ruins are: large finely crafted
blocks that once formed high walls, a considerable geometric mosaic,

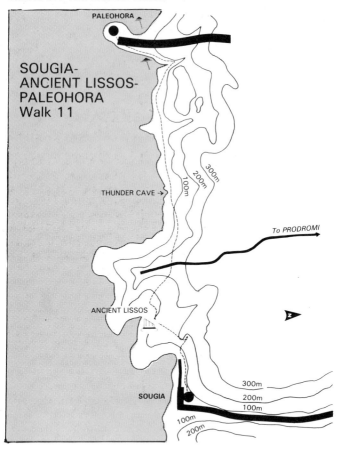

running water and a sewage system throughout the complex. In addition, there were several romanesque votive statues recovered from here that are now on display at the Archaeological Museum in Hania.

Listen closely as you near the valley floor to the trickling sound of spring water and follow the sound to the source. The water emerges from the centre of the complex; it is icy clean, providing a brief respite from the heat. Lissos is not on the itinerary of many

86

A beautiful geometric mosaic awaits your gaze at Ancient Lissos.

travellers, in turn becoming the perfect place for near solitary exploration of another age.

Catch the trail to Paleohora at the only remaining residence in Lissos, near a restored church just uphill from the remains of the asklepieion. The hike to Paleohora is strenuous, but entirely rewarding if you bring enough food and liquids. The trail continues uphill for quite some time after leaving Lissos, eventually levelling off in moonscape-like terrain. Just soon enough the Libyan Sea comes into view, but before thinking too hard about cooling your heels – take a rather long, careful hike downhill. From Lissos to a small cove (Thundercove) with a good spot for swimming and enough space for a couple of tents takes approximately 3 hours. (4½h).

It's yet another 2 hours along the waterfront, across several isolated beaches, to the destination. Paleohora soon comes into clear view. The whitewashed buildings clinging to the peninsula that juts out into the sea. The trail seems to disappear along some of the beaches. At one rocky point it heads inland a short distance before going up and over.

Walking through the orange groves and on to Paleohora is the final reward of the long hike. Plenty of tavernas, restaurants, rooms and even an occasional disco line the streets. The long sandy beach that occupies the entire west side of the peninsula offers year round swimming. There is an official campground that you will pass on the way into town – an important landmark for those taking the hike in reverse. (6½h).

12) FALASARNA

Walking Time: ½ hour to 1½ hours depending on your curiosity.

Access: Take the coastal road west from Hania until reaching Kastelli/Kisamos (42 kms.). Continue along the coastal road which soon angles south to Platanos (53 kms.). Follow the signs to Falasarna 3 kms. away.

Bus Journey Time: 2 hours.
There is bus service every hour during the day from Hania to Kastelli/Kisamos. From this point there are only 2 buses daily to the village of Platanos. From Platanos either walk the remaining 3 kms. to Falasarna or take a local taxi. (Taking a taxi from Kastelli to Falasarna is also a reasonable alternative.

Description: On the far western end of Crete is Falasarna, an area brimming with natural beauty and archaeological excitement. Just below a bluff headland is a series of wide, sandy beaches enclosed by turquoise waters. At the northern edge of the coastal plain are the uplifted remains of a Dorian age port. Once a flourishing Greek city-state, Falasarna is currently being excavated by a team of archaeologists. Many secrets of the site are revealed during a short jaunt along a country road.

The walk can begin anywhere you please due to interconnecting dirt roads. For ease of description, we will begin at the small cluster of two recently built tavernas (with rooms to let), situated above the

DIAGRAM OF UPLIFTED HARBOUR

TIME AND TOPOGRAPHY

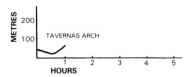

beach on the road from Platanos. Proceed north for 30 min. along a small track through olive groves and many thermokipos (plastic greenhouses) used for banana production. The remains from the first city ever built on this western promontory are visible after the last stretch of beach. This beachfront is perfectly suited for swimming as the white sand reaches far into the water providing soft, sure footing. It is also protected from the wind by a sheer cliff face.

Although ancient writers speak of the artificial port of Falasarna, the best discussion comes from two tireless English travellers that visited the site in the 1800s. Both Captain Spratt and his predecessor, Robert Pashley, write with astonishing clarity about the remains. Their observations are being utilized in the current excavation, along with the aid of modern science. Under the direction of Elpida Hadjidaki, a Cretan, the processes of magnetic, electromagnetic and seismic locating are used to discover underground ruins. It is the first major dig in the area and she explained in patient detail about the surroundings.

Due to local uplift, the ancient port and harbour channels now lay uselessly 6.56 metres above sea level. It is not known if the port area was self serving, or perhaps commanded by the nearby summit city of Polyrinia[1]. There was a large acropolis built on a tip of rock to the northwest of the port area. Barely visible are the Hellenistic terraces that once supported the streets of a city, buildings, a temple and towers. The rough hewn sandstone blocks used as building materials were taken from a large rock quarry to the south of the port. Among the quarry are rock tombs and close by is a large throne cut of solid

---

1. Polyrinia was an important classical Greek city-state built on a commanding position just 7 kms. south of Kastelli. The stronghold had a territory that was said to extend from the northern to the southern sea. There is repeated speculation that Falasarna was a major port for the Polyrinneans, but the 20 km. distance between the sites casts doubt on that observation. Polyrinia was able to take part in wars against Knossos and Gortyna, and many coins attest to its importance around the 5th century B.C.

89

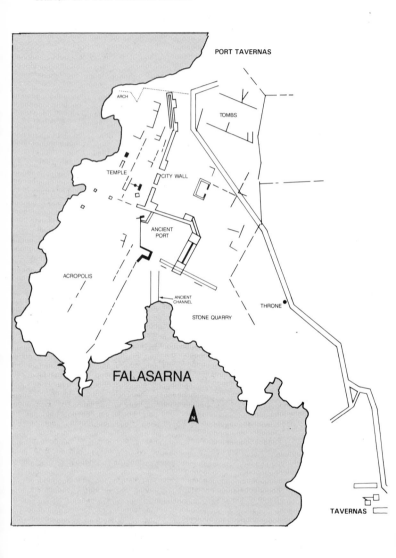

PORT TAVERNAS

ARCH

TOMBS

TEMPLE

CITY WALL

ANCIENT
PORT

ACROPOLIS

ANCIENT
CHANNEL

THRONE

STONE QUARRY

FALASARNA

N

TAVERNAS

stone. The throne is crude and misshapen and it sits much too low for comfort of the legs, while the arms are too high. Perhaps, it was used to honour the Gods, like the thrones erected in Greek temples. Somehow the art of modern fortification was used extensively in this ancient city. Several round bastions (only one is now uncovered) were placed along a line of double walls as a protective measure.

******

Located just 20 metres above sea level on the northern face of the acropolis site, is a hidden gem – thankfully without a shred of historical importance. A small goat path leads uphill for 10 minutes from the best preserved city wall to a spectacular natural rock archway. You may need to exercise some patience in locating it because it is so well hidden, though it is time well spent! (Hint: from the opposite angle it looks only like a deep hole to the sea. Walk carefully around to the other side.) It is a delicate balancing act of nature that allows for a dramatic, framed view into the churning waters below.

13) SPILI – MONASTERY PREVELI – LEFKOGIA

Walking Time: 5¼ hours.

Access: From Rethymnon centre, follow Dimtrakaki street (next to the National Garden) out of town. Continue south for 30 kms. to the village of Spili, where the walk begins. Since it is a one way walk, it will be time consuming to retrieve a car.

Bus Journey Time: ¾ hour.
There is bus service 4 times daily from Rethymnon (originating in Hania) to Agia Galini. Get off the bus before Agia Galini, in the small town of Spili.

Return: The walk ends in the village of Lefkogia on the Plakias – Rethymnon bus route. There are buses 5 times daily along the route from early morning to early evening. A set of current timetables will speed your trip from Lefkogia to the pleasant beachfront setting of Plakias, or back to Rethymnon.

Description: This is a walk for those wanting to explore some of Crete's smaller untouristed villages, during a day trip beginning due south of Rethymnon. It's a rather long walk into a slow pace of life that exists alongside the modern aspects of a changing island. The

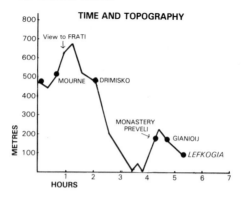

rocky country road twists downhill to the south coast and the palm beach of Limni. After a short jaunt uphill, the road ends at the medieval ambience of the Monastery of Preveli. The trek can be tiring in summer, but an early start will allow time for a midday swim.

The small yet thriving village of Spili is at once appealing to the eyes and senses. Larger than most villages in the vicinity, Spili has a few tavernas, hotel, rooms to let and a market. Flanked by high mountains to the east and rolling hills to the west, the village enjoys a pleasant setting. The memory of cascading water out of a unique fountain in the centre of town is something to preserve for the coming hours across the dry landscape. To accompany the memory it would be a good idea to fill a bottle or canteen and bring it along.

About 100 metres south of Spili, follow a sign indicating a right turn to the village of Mourne. The road dips into a hollow before rising slowly to a good view of Spili. Wind through small plots of land used for growing cereals to feed domestic animals. For your palate, try the plentiful tree-ripened cherries in this area during early summer. In a bit less than ½ hour you will arrive at the sleepy village of Mourne. The pace is so slow here that you should take care not to be overcome by inertia as you pass through. There are four cafés tucked under the many shade trees in town. From the centre, a small cement road (Odos Nikiforada, ask for the road to Drimisko if unsure.) leads uphill for 5 minutes, before reaching a "T" intersection. Turn right on a larger dirt road that leads uphill for 15 minutes more before coming to a ridge.

From the ridge there is a panoramic view into a bowl shaped valley. The road to the right visibly leads downhill to the village of Frati. This

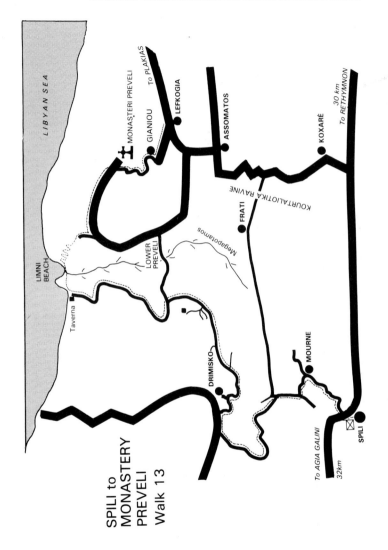

SPILI to
MONASTERY
PREVELI
Walk 13

Exposed and nearly devoid of monks, the Monastery Preveli stands as a monument to its own rich history.

village lies near the yawning opening of the Kourtaliotiko Gorge. (It is possible to walk down to Frati and through the gorge to the main paved road that leads to Preveli. However, we take a slightly longer, seldom used approach.) Just before coming to the ridge, a dirt road leads east (a left turn from Mourne) to the village of Drimisko. There are no signs whatsoever, but it is easy to perceive the main track. (1h).

This road soon reaches a high point where the small town of Drimisko comes into view with the Libyan Sea in the background. From the crucial left turn at the top of the ridge, it takes an hour to reach Drimisko on a degenerating dirt road. Just before reaching the whitewashed village, turn right onto an asphalt road and take another right into the village. Follow the sign indicating Preveli 8 kms.

Drimisko is protected by a long rocky ridge to the north. It is an aesthetic setting, but like so many isolated mountain villages the inhabitants are slowly leaving for the promise of the north coast resorts. The village is ringed by untended olive groves and there is not a taverna or café to be found.

Pass into town and follow the sign indicating Xammoydi, 5 kms., to the right. The road, seen before from above, leads clearly across the barren hills to the west of Drimisko. There is a split in the dirt road about 15 minutes after leaving town. (2h).

Take the left fork (not the other leading uphill) and then stay on the lower road until reaching a hodgepodge junction of 5 roads about 40 minutes out of Drimisko. Pass just to the right of a dirt mound separating the alternatives and take the road that appears to lead to the seaside resort of Plakias. It is this main dirt road that deceptively splits again in a hollow below. The right fork leads behind 3 tall peaks to Plakias, but you will follow to the left on a road that twists down the side of a gully, ending at the sea. You will likely feel out in the middle of nowhere in this area of very few people and inspirational views. Don't fret! In one hour from the intersection at the dirt mound, you will arrive at a remote taverna near a rocky beach. (3h).

From the taverna (rooms to let) there is a sign pointing the way to the palm beach of Limni on a marked footpath. It is only 15 minutes ahead to this isolated oasis, situated at the base of a narrow ravine. There is a fresh water estuary giving life to the many palms and pink oleander that line the ravine. This beach is easily superior to Vai in terms of beauty and isolation. Some 45 years ago, the pebbles of Limni were used to launch a retreat to Egypt by English and Commonwealth soldiers. In these more peaceful times it is simply a nice place to pass a few hours while looking out to the tiny islands of "Paximadia". Aptly named after the hard bread that Cretans dunk in water or milk before eating – follow our advice and avoid the islands and the bread.

The last 1½ hours of walking begins at the west end of the beach on a small marked footpath that leads quickly up the mountainside. The zig-zagging path soon ends in a small dirt road ahead. Turn left on the paved road and before long the monastery comes into view. (4½h).

With a spectacular position 170 metres above the Libyan Sea, many monks once enjoyed the seclusion of Monastery Preveli. Today the barren landscape offers more solitude that the Abbot Spitadakis and the last remaining monk yearn for. With the pious activity of prior ages gone forever, the monastery lives on with memories of its revolutionary past.

Like many Cretan monasteries, several uprisings against the Turks (1669 – 1898) were staged from the protective isolation of Preveli. This infuriated the occupying force to the point where the monastery was sacked and burned to the ground. Preveli was eventually rebuilt and was able to continue its role in the struggle against the Turks.

More recently, the walled courtyard served as a holding area for retreating allied soldiers. The escape to Egypt was carried out by submarines that were loaded below at the beachhead Limni. There are grateful commemorative plaques attesting to the sympathetic aid of the Monastery.

The sign on the front gate asks people to dress respectably and not to wear shorts. A caretaker is on call during the daylight hours and he will be happy to give a brief tour of the grounds. Inside the church is a cross said to contain a fragment of the true cross. There is also a small museum displaying other relics and highly decorative robes. Another important feature of the monastery is the central fountain built in 1701 with the Greek inscription: "Wash your sins not only your face". Cool spring water flows out for those interested in either. The setting and history of Preveli are now preserved, but the eerie feeling of the abandoned lower monastery (seen from the main auto route 2 kms. away) is fast encroaching.

Since there is no direct bus service from the Monastery of Preveli, we have outlined a 45 minute jaunt to the village of Lefkogia on the Plakias – Rethymnon bus route. At the junction of the road leading into Preveli and the parking area, a footpath leads up the dry hillside. (A road was under construction and may now be completed.) Turn left onto the path and in 10 minutes there is a ridge which marks the last uphill portion. Lead down the other side on a small dirt road that soon reveals the village of Gianiou. Just after a stone and concrete housed spring, turn right onto a stepped cement path leading down to Gianiou. After passing through the tiny village, continue downhill on the main asphalt road for 15 minutes. Turn left on the road to Plakias and in 5 minutes the journey ends in Lefkogia (rooms, tavernas, mini-market). (5h 15m).

14) THRONOS – MONASTERY ARKADI

Walking Time: 2 hours.

Access: From the National Garden in Rethymnon, take Kountourioti Street east for 3 km. before the road splits. Take the right fork and head south following the signs to Amari and crossing the new coastal road. The asphalt road rises steadily until reaching Agia Fotini (30 km. Turn left going through the village and in 1 km. turn left on the small road that angles back to Thronos (32 km.).

Majestic Mount Koussakas on the descent from the Nida Plateau.
(Nida to Voriza - Option 2, Walk 16)

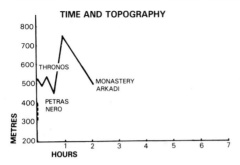

Bus Journey Time: 45 minutes.
There is bus service 3 times daily on the Rethymnon – Amari route. Be sure to specify to the bus
attendant that you are going to Thronos. The bus
does not stop in Thronos, but at a nearby
intersection shortly after Agia Fotini.

Return: There are 4 buses daily from the Monastery of
Arkadi to Rethymnon.

Description: Beginning at the small village of Thronos at the head
of the fertile Amari Valley is an excursion back to medieval Crete.
Thronos recalls the now faded glory of the Byzantine era through its
frescoes and partial mosaic floor. From its mountainous setting, a
country road leads easily to more recent foundations of Cretan
history. The fortified Monastery of Arkadi is the supreme symbol of
Cretan resistance against the Turks and the bitter dilemma of all
Cretans: freedom or death.

From the marked junction where the bus stops, walk 10 minutes
uphill along a paved road to Thronos (rooms, taverna). The small
village looks out over a valley full of apple, pear, cherry, kumkwat
and, of course, olive trees. But the locale is dominated from the east
by Crete's tallest peak, Psiloritis (2456 m, see Walk 16). Thronos was
once the site of an ancient Hellenistic township named Sybritos, but
the current name is derived from early Byzantium. Upon entering
town, remains from this era can be seen in a once large mosaic that is
now partially expunged by the church built atop it. Inside of the stone
church are sombre yet carefully painted frescoes, from later
Byzantium.

Follow the road through Thronos to the north. Soon you will be
hemmed in by rolling hills in a rural setting. Pass by the tiny village of

Left: At the summit of Psiloritis two women light candles and incense 97
for the chapel. (Walk 17)

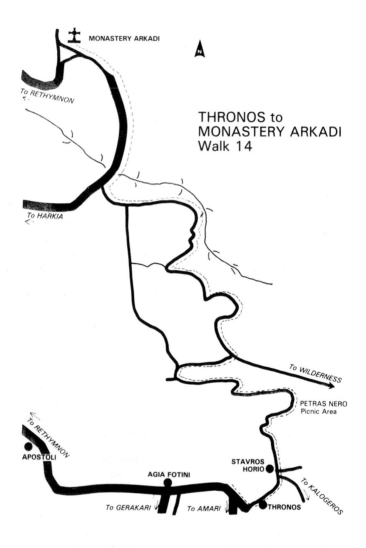

MONASTERY ARKADI

To RETHYMNON

To HARKIA

THRONOS to MONASTERY ARKADI Walk 14

To WILDERNESS

PETRAS NERO
Picnic Area

To RETHYMNON

APOSTOLI

AGIA FOTINI

STAVROS
HORIO

To KALOGEROS

To GERAKARI

To AMARI

THRONOS

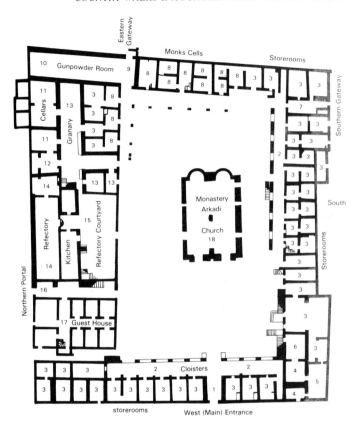

MONASTERY ARKADI

1. Main (West) Entrance
2. Cloisters
3. Storerooms
4. Cheese-making Cell
5. Wine Cellar
6. Olive Oil Cellar
7. Southern Gateway
8. Monks' Cells
9. Eastern Gateway
10. Gunpowder Room
11. Cellars
12. Kitchen
13. Granary
14. Refectory
15. Refectory Courtyard
16. Northern Portal
17. Guest House
18. Monastery Arkadi Church

Stavros Horio and, in half an hour, you will arrive at a shaded spring next to the road. The water (petras nero) is rumoured to cure kidney ailments with its medicinal qualities. At any rate, there are a few benches and it is a nice place for a break or even a picnic. The gray road rising on the other side of the valley proceeds to your destination. (30 mins).

From the spring, it is 30 minutes of uphill walking along a dirt road to reach a "T" intersection. Take a left turn leading past a field of ferns, and a lonely tree, towards a soon visible Arkadi. (A right turn will land you in a beautiful and remote wilderness setting near the base of Psiloritis in just over an hour.) The dirt track leads along a gully floor, emerging in 45 minutes at the main gravel road to Arkadi. Turn right, and walk 10 minutes through impressive pine trees situated along golden fields of grain. (2h).

The façade of the church at the Monastery of Arkadi has an ornamental detachment from the rest of the fortified grounds. Built by the Venetians, Arkadi's immortality came from its near destruction on November 9, 1866. In an isolated position high above Rethymnon, the monastery served as a centre of resistance for the ongoing struggle against Turkish rule. In late 1866 a large group of guerrillas, as well as women and children, had gathered themselves in the Monastery. Turkish troops attacked the stronghold and when those inside refused to surrender, thousands of additional troops were called in. Defeat became imminent as the Turkish assailants entered the fortified walls, but at the same moment a defender torched the powder magazine. The resulting explosion killed hundreds and possibly thousands of Cretans and Turks alike.

A small museum on the grounds has remnants of Arkadi's turbulent history. Outside the thick walls of the courtyard is a monument with busts of the "heroes" of 1866, and skulls of other unfortunates. The anniversary of the event is marked by a solemn observance that attracts a large crowd from Crete and the rest of Greece.

When you are ready to move on to other topics, try a bowl of yogurt with local thyme honey at the small taverna out front. There is balcony seating in the cool pine-scented air of the mountains.

Monastery Arkadi.

15) VRISES – GOURGOUTHI & PAINTED CHURCHES IN THE AMARI VALLEY

Walking Time: 1¼ hours.

Access: Take the main road east from the National Gardens in Rethymnon towards Iraklion for 3 km. Take the right fork crossing the new road and follow the signs to Amari. The road will then cross a broad ridge offering a vista to the valley ahead. Drive through Apostoli (30 km.) and 1 km. further, turn rght at the "T" intersection in Agia Fotini. The road leads past Meronas (34 km.) and Gerakari (41 km.) before reaching the starting point at Vrises (45 km.). Do not stop at the churches during the last couple of kilometres before Vrises, as the walk will soon bring you back this way.

Since this short walk requires personal transportation, a tour of other Amari Valley churches may easily be taken. Other fine examples of frescoed churches may be found in the nearby villages of Agia Paraskevi, Vorizia, and Fourfouras.

Description: God is nowhere forgotten as you pass by the startling number of churches and chapels in the Amari Valley. This fertile area possesses some of the finest frescoed churches in Crete. The walk begins at the village of Vrises. Upon entering, to the west of town, a small road can be seen which branches off to the right. After only 30 metres, a cobblestone path forks up the hillside under the shade of four tall cypress trees. This visible path leads uphill for 20 minutes to the tiny settlement of Gourgouthi. As you get close to the village, the trail becomes somewhat overgrown, but never too difficult.

The hamlet of Gourgouthi is beginning to be excluded from most maps of the island. Tucked away in the trees, it is an age-old reminder of simpler ways, and longer hours. The two remaining year-round residents invited us in for a lingering chat. As we traded stories, an older shepherd on a mule rode right in. A blackened copper kettle to the side was filled with newly made canes. Simply, knotted sticks which had been heated until pliable. One end is then bent around a stone and secured until it sets into a crook. Follow through the surprisingly well kept summer homes, and pass by a

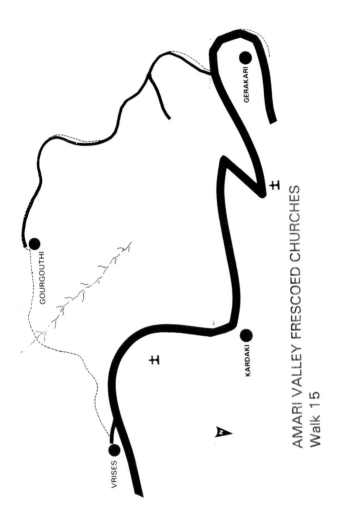

AMARI VALLEY FRESCOED CHURCHES
Walk 15

spring as you leave on the only dirt road. Turn right and point yourself back to Vrises. (1h).

Only 10 minutes after setting out on the small asphalt road, is the unusual architecture of Agios Ioannis Theologos. Inside the exposed side chapel are 13th century frescoes, with slightly newer frescoes in the narthex. Since early Byzantium, paintings inside the churches have followed a predetermined order. In front of the church is a shaded seating area with a cold spring water tap. It is a good place from which to admire the setting, between the imposing slopes of Mount Kedros (1777 m.) to the south and Psiloritis (2456 m.) to the east. Continue along the paved road to the east to the village of Kardaki. Just a few minutes beyond, lying low in a field of grain, is another frescoed chapel. Give the sticky door some prompting for a glance at some carefully painted frescoes in the altar area. The walking loop is soon completed at Vrises only 10 minutes away. (1h 15m).

16) PSILORITIS SUMMIT & OPTIONAL DESCENTS

Walking Time: 8 hours along the most basic route, longer options are discussed.

Access: From the Hania Gate in Iraklion, follow the road that proceeds westward along the coast. Pass by the road to Festos in 2 km. and proceed along the main road. In 11 km. turn left onto a smaller asphalt road to Tilisos (14 km.), Gonies (25 km.), and up to the village of Anogia (35 km.). A still smaller road (good enough for a car) winds its way to the Nida Plateau, where the hike begins and ends.

Bus Journey Time: 1 hour.
There is a bus service twice daily from Rethymnon and 6 times daily from Iraklion to Anogia. To reach the starting point of the hike from Anogia, there are a couple of possibilities:

1) Start walking along the road to the Nida Plateau, and hitchhike along the way. In summer, there are cars making the trip and someone will likely stop if they have room. If not, it will take 4 hours of steady walking to reach Nida, 20 kms.

TIME AND TOPOGRAPHY

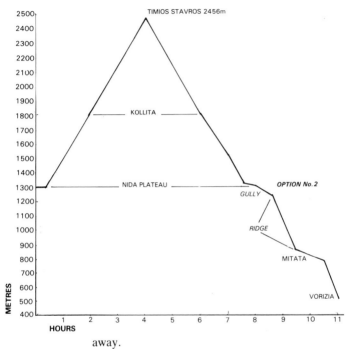

away.

2) Ask around in Anogia for a "local taxi" to the Nida Plateau. Someone is bound to be making the trip anyway, and a few drachmas may be just the right incentive to take it now, instead of later.

Description: For a worthwhile adventure, how about a hike to the top of the tallest peak on Crete? Although it requires plenty of strength and endurance, it is not as difficult as it may sound. The mountain, called Psiloritis (2456 metres) presides over Crete's entirety like a sleeping giant. (It is also called Mount Ida, but not the classically famous one of Homer.) Enshrouded in mythology, history – and very often clouds – it is the natural beauty of Psiloritis' vast contours that lure people to the summit. There are many possible routes that we will mention, but only one will be discussed in detail. The basic path begins and ends in the alpine plain of Nida, taking a

105

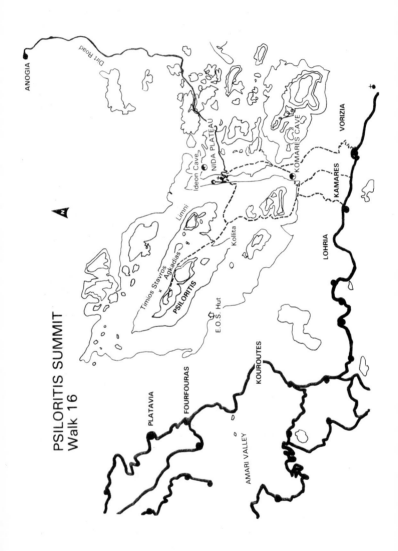

PSILORITIS SUMMIT
Walk 16

full 8 hours to complete. It can be done in a long day of hiking, but a night on top, embraced by both sunset and sunrise, is absolutely unforgettable. Just be certain to bring enough food, water, warm clothing – and any necessary camping gear for a cold overnight. There is questionable cistern water near the summit chapel of Timios Stavros (Holy Cross) – we drank some without consequence.

Assuming you have reached the Nida Plain, (no services) the summit approach begins at the far west side. Sitting all alone next to the main road is the starkly modern and now abandoned Ideon Andron Taverna. Follow a small road on the opposite side uphill, passing a spring and a whitewashed chapel, a red waymarking directs you onto the footpath. If you are interested in seeing the Ideon Cave, continue up the road for 10 minutes before returning to this point.

The cave was discovered in the late 1880s, and it immediately provided a notable Dorian find of ornamental bronze shields with skilled relief work. Other finds in a small cave near the back include: bronze vessels, tripods, sphinxes, spears, lamps, and bronze figurines of humans and animals. (Now on display in the Iraklion Archaeological Museum.) The contents of the large cave (length 40 m, width 35 m, height 60 m) seem to indicate a cult worshiping of the Kuretes. They were the warriors that shouted loudly and clashed their shields to drown the cries of the newborn Zeus. This was to protect him from being eaten by his father, Kronos, who had swallowed all previous sons and daughters. The 9th and 8th century B.C. finds have provided fuel for the scholarly debate of just where the imaginary Zeus was born and raised – the Ideon Cave, or the Dikteon Cave (see Walk 17), or some place altogether different.

The footpath leads south in a parallel manner with the road across Nida that is visible below. The trail is fairly easy to spot as it tracks levelly along the mountainside. In about ½ hour there is a dramatic shift in the direction and grade of the trail. Follow the red dots across a gully between two mountains. Continue steadily uphill on the rocky path for 1¼ hours before reaching a high point next to a small stone shelter. From here there are good views back to Nida and uphill to Koussakas Peak (2211 metres). DO NOT follow the tempting red arrows uphill from this point, or you will climb Mount Koussakas and not Psiloritis. (1h 45m).

It is crucial to head downhill from the small shelter. Turn left and follow the ridge downhill in a southerly direction – infrequent stone piles and red waymarkings show the way. In just 15 minutes you reach a merging of trails in the basin of Kollita. It is possible to spend the night here in the event of bad weather. It is fairly protected and

A cart track to the north-west of Psiloritis, (2,456m).

there are several Mitata (stone huts, built igloo style) nearby and springwater. From the halfway point of Kollita turn right (northwest) and proceed gradually uphill on an obvious and well marked trail. (A left turn will take you down to the Kamares Cave and, on a steep route, to the town of the same name – see Kamares option.)

The barren landscape seems to continue for a long time during this point of the ascent. The surrounding landform is deceptive as to the high elevation of the area. It isn't until 1½ hours from Kollita, with the first sight of the Mediterranean, that you realise just how high you are. But the summit still hasn't come into sight! It is not until the final 20 minutes of the ascent that the tallest point in Crete, Timios Stavros, lends itself to clear view. Follow the ridge uphill and enjoy the incredible panorama from the top (4h).

We didn't meet anyone during our hike along this route and were therefore quite surprised by the 15 or so people already on the summit. It was a friendly group from E.O.S. (Greek Mountaineering Club) that had made their annual hike together. After offering their congratulations, they asked us to join them in a veritable feast of meatballs, dolmathes, fresh fruits and vegetables, and loaves of bread. We put forth our meager offerings and, by the nature of the conversation, began to realise just how lucky we were that this day was without a strong wind and without clouds.

About halfway through the meal, two starchy women in their 70s appeared on the horizon. They were dressed all in black and had made the ascent in a mere 2½ hours from Nida, along a different route. Upon arrival, they quickly opened their satchels and pulled out candles and incense before disappearing inside the Chapel of the Holy Cross (Timios Stavros). Soon the air was scented by incense that found its way through the spaces in the stones. A peek inside the tiny chapel was glorified by 10 – 15 lighted candles.

The group left in the early afternoon and only a few holders-on were there to gaze out over the lingering sunset. The intense colours seemed to hang timelessly in the air before making way for the cold moonless night.

The trip back is – unremarkably – much like the hike up, except perhaps a bit quicker. After 1½ hours there is a bright red cross painted on the rocks to indicate a junction of trails at the sheepfold, Kollita. Turn left and follow uphill along a ridge on the Nida route. (The right fork leads downhill to Kamares – see the Kamares option below.) The ridge leads uphill for 15 minutes to a view of the Nida Plain next to a stone shelter. Follow down the right side of the gully and be careful to watch for a red triangle denoting a splitting of trails. Take the left trail that crosses the gully and leads along the side of the plain from far above. In ½ hour you will arrive at the cool spring water where the trek began. (8h).

* * * * * *

OPTIONS FOR THE ASCENT/DESCENT OF PSILORITIS

1. *Kollita Basin – Kamares Cave – Kamares*

From the junction of trails at Kollita, 1½ hours from the summit of Psiloritis, it is possible to reach the cave of Kamares and the town of the same name. It is a strenuous route taking the right fork from Kollita down the steep southern face of Psiloritis. It is a well marked trail that allows for beautiful views to the Libyan Sea, but you will need to keep your eyes locked on the trail. In about 3 hours there is spring water near a merging trail that leads east to the Kamares cave (length 70 m, width 60 m, height 80 m). In the early 1900s the British excavated the cave to find striking examples of sculptured Minoan pottery done in the polychrome style. The delicate workmanship of Kamares Ware represents the first great period of Minoan pottery. (Many examples of Kamares Ware may be seen in the Archaeological Museum in Iraklion.) After visiting the cave backtrack to the trail that descends steeply to the village of Kamares in 3 hours or continue straight from the cave and turn right on another marked, steep trail leading to the same destination.

2.   Nida — Vorizia
This walk begins at the south end of Nida on a spectacular wilderness route that takes 3–4 hours. Due to trail finding difficulties, this unmarked route should only be attempted by experienced and well prepared hikers. There is no water whatsoever in this extremely isolated area. From Nida, drop down into a gully that evolves into a severe ravine thick with trees. (DO NOT follow the glaring red arrows at the top of the ravine or you will take option number 3 to Kamares.)

The stream bed is passable except for a few overgrown places, where there is a circumventing trail. After the first hour, the trail rises to the left shoulder of the new confined ravine. (If you miss the trail leading to the left side there will be a greeting of tumbledown boulders that are difficult to negotiate. The going is never too rough – if it is, you've gone too far down the ravine. Backtrack to reach the trail that runs above the ravine to the east (on the left side from the top).) Follow along the shaded path and savour the views to the Messara Plain, the Paximadia Islands, back up to the Koussakas side of Psiloritis and down into the deep ravine just beside (beware of vertigo!).

It is another hour of walking along the east side of the cleft to a crucial left turn. This occurs when the trail emerges on a wide open ridge among a myriad of goat paths. DO NOT continue straight ahead. Turn left, away from the ravine you have been paralleling, and make your way to the east. There is a trail that runs by a pine tree and then overlooks a smaller ravine with a shepherd's mitato on the opposite side. The trail skirts the top opening and runs behind the mitato with some animal troughs just below. The path resumes at the water troughs and switches steeply downhill to a dirt road and finally Vorizia (taverna, rooms).

3.   Nida – Kamares
From the south end of Nida follow the red arrows onto a marked (though faded) trail that leads close to the Kamares cave and on to the village of Kamares in approximately 6 hours. The route is very steep, but the views are beautiful. There is no water along this route.

4.   Ascent from the Amari Valley
The Amari Valley is a beautiful area from which to stage an ascent up

110

the western side of Psiloritis. There are several possible routes from the villages of Vistagi (via the road to the sheepfold of Chikalas), Kouroutes, Fourfouras, and Lohria. From each of the small villages a dirt road marks the beginning of the ascent, but there is no trail for the remainder of the way. It is not terribly difficult to orient yourself to the visible summit, but the environment is a bit hostile (many varieties of thistle and thorny plants – and the shale rocks make the footing unsure). Otherwise, the views over the western end of the island make it worth your while.

The Rethymnon E.O.S. (Greek Mountaineering Club) has built a hut on a spectacular perch that is accessible from the west.

17) LASSITHI PLAIN – DIKTEON CAVE

Walking Time:	1 hour from Agios Georgios to the Dikteon Cave.
Access:	1) There is easy access to Lassithi from either Iraklion (along a more dramatic route) or Agios Nicholaos. From Iraklion follow the coastal road east for 23 kms. before turning right towards Potamis (34 kms.), Avdou and eventually down to the plain. Follow the ring road clockwise to Tzermiado and continue on to Agios Georgios (58 kms.).

Bus Journey Time: 2 hours.
There is bus service from Iraklion twice daily, with three buses returning daily from Lassithi.

2) From Agios Nicholaos take the new road in a westerly direction until the town of Neapolis (15 kms.). Follow the signs indicating Lassithi through Vrises, Zenia, Mesa Potami and down to the plain at Mesa Lassithi (40 kms.). Follow the ring road clockwise to Agios Georgios (45 kms.).

Bus Journey Time: 1½ hours.
There are 2 buses daily from Agios Nicholaos and 2 returning from Lassithi.

Description: The lush upland plain of Lassithi lies at an elevation of 850 metres and is a delightful contrast to the rest of Crete. It is beautiful to see thousands of cloth sailed windmills doing cartwheels in the wind. The cloth sails are unfurled only in mid-to-late summer. The plain is 8 – 10 kms. long and 4 – 6 kms. wide, providing some of the richest farmland on Crete. We have outlined an easy walk

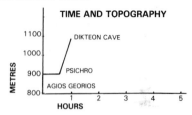

beginning at the town of Agios Georgios. A small country track crosses the plain revealing a way of life barely altered by the forces of time and technology. Eventually the road turns upward onto one of Lassithi's surrounding mountains, ending at the mythological birthplace of Zeus.

Unlike some of the towns along the ring road of the plain, Agios Georgios doesn't pander to tourists. There are a couple of very low key hotels and restaurants alongside a high density of kafeneions (cafés) par capita. For the older men of the town, life revolves around the nucleus of the kafeneion. Traditional Cretan attire is fairly common among the older generation. The looks you receive are intense as you pass through town, but they will break into an easy smile and wave, once spoken to. A simple "Yassas!" is a formal greeting that can be used to crack their tough exteriors.

Agios Georgios is home to a very good folklore museum (hours: 10-4, Mon.– Fri.). There are signs directing you from the main street to a small group of buildings that serve as a museum. Captured inside are the simple everyday implements of a village house. Thoreau would have been overjoyed to see that his cabin near Walden Pond could barely match the uncluttered usefulness presented here. How, with the wine press handily stored below the bed, could there be a better use of space? The other rooms provide glimpses of life and art on Crete with displays of paintings, pictures, weaving and an area devoted to Nikos Kazantakis' life.

From the museum back to the main street, walk through town past the schoolyard and Hotel Rea in a westerly direction. The road quickly becomes the rutted dirt variety that cuts across the fertile soil of the plain. The dirt road parallels the deep irrigation channels that have been used since Venetian times. Oddly enough, after the Venetians had fully irrigated the plain, they relocated the entire population of Lassithi. Since it is cut off by encircling mountains they were unable to control the inhabitants and expelled everyone for 150 years. Yet the fertility of the area eventually could not be denied and

112

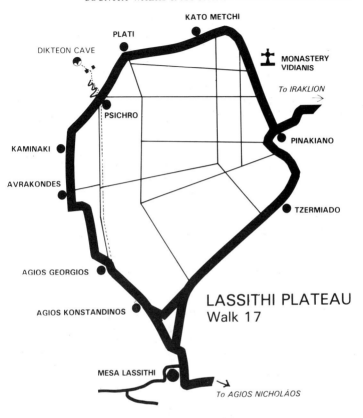

the plain was reopened for farming. Today, there are 21 villages located on the periphery of the plain, freeing up the best land for the cultivation of potatoes, grain and fruit. The bustle of rural activity is everywhere during the ½ hour from Agios Georgios to Psichro. (30m).

Continue through the shops and tavernas of Psichro on the ring road before climbing uphill on a marked asphalt road. Complete one switchback and leave the asphalt, passing below Kronos Taverna and then upwards on a stepped cobblestone track towards the cave. The next 30 minutes involves a climb of 200 metres to Zeus' birthplace.

113

To be honest, the excursion to the cave from Psichro is not exactly off the beaten track, but it is worth the trip. The view of the plain is wonderful from above as the ancient lake bed comes into clear focus. Mules may be hired for the ascent to the cave and a guide with a powerful flashlight will accompany you (at a negotiated fee) inside the deep cavern. It gets cool in the depths even in summer, so it's not a bad idea to bring along a light sweater.

It is one of the most vivid Greek Myths that tells the story of the birth of Zeus to Rhea and Kronos, the Lord of the Universe. It was Kronos who took precautions against being overthrown by one of his children, by eating them as they were born. To hide the birth of baby Zeus, a terrified Rhea climbed deep into a cavern to give birth, while her helpers, the Kuretes, danced and shouted wildly to drown the cries of the newborn. Still, Kronos learned of the birth and demanded Rhea give the baby up. Instead, she offered him a stone wrapped in swaddling which he swallowed without hesitation. The baby Zeus was then taken to a different cave and brought up by the goat, Amaltheia.

The cave where Zeus was said to have been born is still under dispute (scholars argue primarily about the Dikteon cave and the Ideon cave on Mount Psiloritis). The hundreds of votive offerings found in Dikteon cave prove that there was a large cult following, that likely reached its peak around 800 B.C. The excavation of these objects took place in 1900 with British and local cooperation. As you climb down the wide gash aided by lights or candles, the inner depths are revealed. Surrounded by large stalactites and stalagmites, the otherworldliness makes it easy to think of the myths – and the cults that followed.

18) LIMNES LOOP

Walking Time: 1½ hours.

Access: From Agios Nicholaos follow the new north coast highway towards Iraklion. Follow the signs directing you onto the old highway before arriving in Limnes (12 kms.).

Bus Journey Time: 15 minutes.
There are frequent buses from Agios Nichlaos to Limnes – take the Iraklion bus and specify that you are getting off in Limnes.

Description: Down in a hollow beside the new north coast highway,

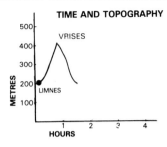

only 12 kms. west of Agios Nichlaos, is unpretentious Limnes. The village consists of closely packed homes interconnected by a maze of narrow alleyways. Leading into carefully tended gardens on the outskirts is a cart track, that eventually winds its way up to the hillside village of Vrises. There, the Monastery Kremaston provides ample shade for a midway break and expansive views to the valley below. It is an intimate journey back in time to a few Cretan villages that remain disentangled from the ornaments of the nearby tourist trade.

Limnes is dominated from the north by rows of thick stone towers that until recently were used for milling corn. Rounded on the windward side and minus their sails, they now appear as useless monuments. To the south are much smaller versions that still bring water for the groves of almond, carob and olive trees that are planted next to vegetable plots. Slender stone and metal towers stand above the trees with painstakingly patched cloth sails unfurled during the drying heat of summer.

From the bus stop on the new road, cross under the highway towards the red roofs of Limnes. Weave down narrow streets to reach the main asphalt road and turn right (west). After passing the last of the cafés take the first left turn. It is a small cement track that crosses a bridge, before leading into the fields. There are a couple of jigs in the road, but keep straight on between stone walls. The track emerges near the cathedral in Houmeriakos (15m). The first major turn left onto a smaller road conducts you past a church. It turns into a cement road. Keep left and plod uphill for a couple of minutes until reaching a dirt footpath that connects to a larger dirt road above. Turn right on the dirt road and in 10 minutes of easy walking, come to a whitewashed chapel raised onto a stone foundation. Take the left fork at the chapel and keep on uphill. In another 10 minutes turn right and walk for 5 minutes to a stepped cobblestone path leading to Vrises (see map for a shortcut). (45m).

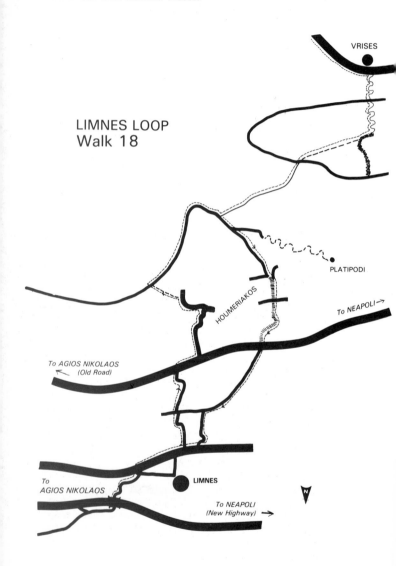

LIMNES LOOP
Walk 18

VRISES

PLATIPODI

To NEAPOLI→

HOUMERIAKOS

To AGIOS NIKOLAOS
(Old Road)
←

To AGIOS NIKOLAOS
←

LIMNES

N

To NEAPOLI
(New Highway) →

The last remaining monk at the Monastery Kremaston stands in front of the church.

117

The cobblestones arrive at Vrises near the lower edge of the thriving village at a rather conspicuous shrine. (It is a good reference point for the return trip.) Venture uphill into the convoluted streets that are stepped out of necessity. Like Limnes, the houses are built closely together to provide a natural defence against invaders. Eventually you will come to main street, where a host of cafés serve a forgotten generation of old men. A few still wear a colourful, if tattered, traditional dress that is unique to Crete. Baggy "Berber-like" trousers are worn with black knee-length boots, while an embroidered vest and a brightly coloured cummerbund stand out against their white puffy blouses. Wrapped loosely around their heads is the black fringe saraci.

Turn left (east) on main street to reach the Monastery Kremaston in 5 minutes. For those with picnic foresight there is a pleasant seating area next to the compound. The last remaining monk will facilitate the short tour of the church and grounds. A small donation is in order. During our visit he continually lamented the fact that all of the finest icons were stolen from the church 10 years ago.

The return walk takes the same route for a short distance before switching tracks. Follow back to the shrine at the head of the cobblestone path and work your way down to the chapel built onto the stone foundation. Keep to the left of the chapel on a wide, and slightly overgrown, pathway. This route enters Houmeriakos from above on a different ridge. Follow down through the village on stepped cement. At one point there is a "T", turn right and angle down to the main road. On the opposite side is a cart track that plots a route back through the fertile greenery ending in Limnes in 15 minutes. (1h 30m).

19) KRITSA – PANAGIA KERA – ANCIENT LATO

Walking Time: 1 hour, allow equal time for return.

Access: Follow a road to the edge of Agios Nicholaos as if going to Ierapetra/Sitia. Continue across the main intersection of the coastal road, and follow the signs up into the foothills to Kritsa.

Bus Journey Time: ½ hour.
There are buses nearly every hour during the day to and from Kritsa.

Description: The village of Kritsa is tucked away in the mountains just 12 km. away from Agios Nicholaos. The town enjoys a

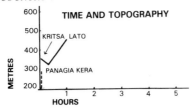

spectacular view over the Gulf of Mirabello from its perch on the steep mountainside. This 1 hour walk treads easily through the endless olive groves below, to a couple of historically diverse sites. The church of Panagia Kera (All Holy Lady) contains some of the finest Byzantine frescoes on Crete, while on down the road are the extensive Dorian ruins of Lato.

From the main square (bus stop) it is worth your while to explore the narrow streets of Kritsa. It takes only a short while to observe that Kritsa has much more to offer than its traditional handicrafts (mostly woven items, and hand worked leather and jewellery). For instance, the procession of villagers coming home after a day in the fields. The preferred method of travel is still the donkey, on which the women somehow manage to look comfortable riding sidesaddle. The peasant dress is traditional and many of the women wear scarves around their head and face to protect from the wind. Open your eyes to a way of life that is a world away from the bric-a-brac that lines main street. There are several places to rent a room for the night, as well as tavernas and small markets.

From the main square, walk east 1 km. back along the same road that comes from Agios Nicholaos. Only 15 minutes just to the side of the main road lies the church of Panagia Kera. Surrounded by a backdrop of Cypress trees and encircled by low walls, the whitewashed structure has a stunted central tower and a separate bell tower. The three naves of the church are covered in rich frescoes from the 14th and 15th centuries. There is a definite sense of strength from the intense figures lining the walls, that leave lasting impressions on those who enter.

Leaving the chapel, follow a small dirt path that leads between the outdoor seating of two tavernas. This narrow road passes through the villagers' gardens for 15 minutes before reaching a larger dirt road. Turn right as the sign indicates and enjoy an easy country stroll to the ancient city of Lato – 30 minutes away. Just before reaching the site, the road splits. Take the right fork past a shrine and on up the hill.

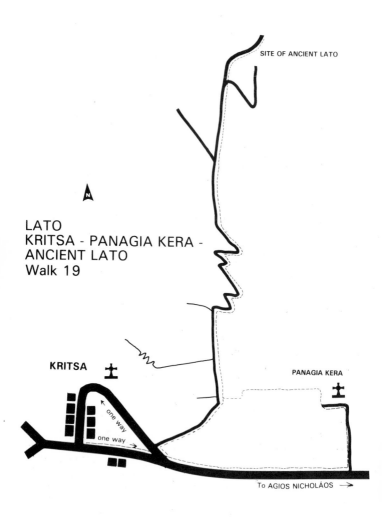

SITE OF ANCIENT LATO

LATO
KRITSA - PANAGIA KERA -
ANCIENT LATO
Walk 19

KRITSA

PANAGIA KERA

one way

one way

To AGIOS NICHOLÁOS →

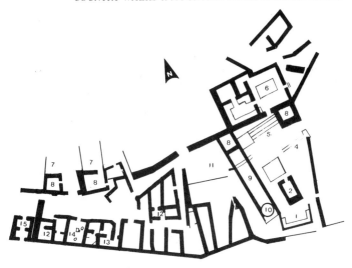

LATO

1. Theatre
2. Temple
3. Cistern
4. Market
5. Stepped Seats
6. Prytaneion
7. Terraced Housing
8. Tower
9. Corridor
10. Threshing Stone
11. Grave
12. Shop
13. House with Handmill
14. Dyehouse
15. City Gate

The lower road leads all the way down to the village of Flamouriana. (1h).

Lato is an extensive set of remains from a flourishing Dorian city that dates back to the 8th century B.C. Lato is a terrific place to unlock the past with new surprises at every turn. The French have excavated the city from the early 1900s and are still turning up finds. The city was built on a saddle looking out towards Agios Nicholaos just 5 km. away.

Massive stone blocks form the high walls and doorways of houses and shops situated along a central road. The stronghold has an agora (market place) that likely served as a public meeting place. Due to the threat of war the water cistern was located in the middle of this public area. A wide tier of steps leads to the 3rd century B.C. Hellenistic remains of a small temple. For all of the trouble to build this protected city, it was peace that eventually secured its demise. The inhabitants began resettling on the coast because Lato was too difficult to reach. By Roman times the city was abandoned. Though devoid of inhabitants, Lato still possesses its principal charm; a panoramic view over the foothills to the coast and the Gulf of Mirabello.

20) EPISKOPI – THRIPTI – KAVOUSI

Walking Time:	4 hours.
Access:	Episkopi is close to both Agios Nicholaos and Ierapetra. From Agios Nicholaos take the coastal road east (towards Sitia) passing the Minoan site of Gournia in 19 kms. Turn right at 22 kms. and follow the signs towards Ierapetra, soon reaching Episkopi (30 kms.). From Ierapetra it is only a 5 km. northerly jaunt to Episkopi.
	Bus Journey Time: 5 min. from Ierapetra. 45 min. from Agios Nicholaos. Nearly every hour throughout the day there is bus service to Episkopi on the Agios Nicholaos – Ierapetra run (and vice-verse).
Return:	There are 6 daily buses from Kavousi to Agios Nicholaos (Sitia bus). A return to Ierapetra requires a bus change in Pachia Ammos – check in advance for a timetable.

Description: Merely 5 kms. from the largest south coast town of Ierapetra (population 11,000), begins an exhilarating day trip in quiet Episkopi. The road that connects both coasts of Crete at its narrowest point cuts through the middle of Episkopi. Only on foot, however, can its many charms be reached. Leading into the Thripti Mountains is a country track that serves up expansive views to the north and south coasts. Once encircled by the vineyards of the still smaller hamlet of Thripti, a smaller path, cobblestoned in places, shows the way down to Kavousi, with a stunning panorama to the north.

Episkopi is the largest of the 4 villages clustered about the base of the Thripti Mountains near the northern tip of the Ierapetra Plain. The walk begins below the main road at a bewildering medieval

TIME AND TOPOGRAPHY

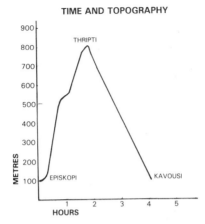

church opposite the village centre. (Above the paved road is the cathedral, the town square and several cafés.) The north nave of the church is surmounted by a Byzantine dome, while the other side is built in Venetian style. Under the 13th century dome of Agios Georgios the Greek Orthodox community worshipped; just beside them, in Agios Karalambos, under a pitched roof, was the Catholic congregation.

Beginning at this gem of Byzantium is a small cement road that plots a course through the fields to Epanohori (upper village). A couple of minutes after setting out, the road comes to a "T". Turn right and then angle left over a small bridge to reach the outskirts of Epanohori in 5 minutes. Keep on until meeting a grouping of well-shaded cafés – no doubt the nucleus of village life for the men. Many are seated in a row drinking tiny cups of Greek coffee or quite possibly strong shots of "raki" (sometimes called tsikoudia) with "mezes" (appetisers of cucumber or watermelon in summer; wild artichoke suffices in winter time). At this social conglomeration there is a small sign directing you onto the road to Thripti. Go ahead and ask which way if unsure because help is readily forthcoming despite any language barriers.

Walk past curious village scenes towards the silver dome of the cathedral. From there, a dirt road leads gradually up the mountain-side, reaching an out of place Georgian style chapel in 20 minutes. The road continues uphill offering an ever widening vista back to the plastic sea of greenhouses beside Ierapetra, and to the north coast.

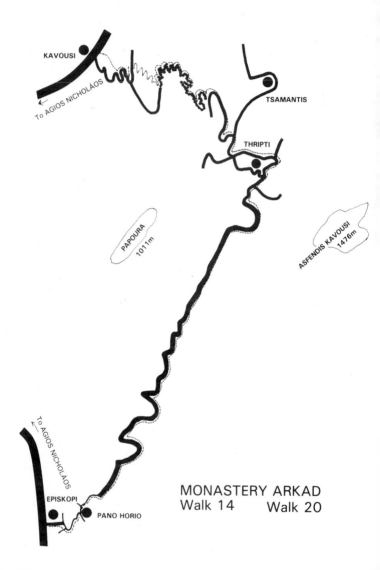

KAVOUSI

To AGIOS NICHOLÁOS

TSAMANTIS

THRIPTI

PAPOURA
1011m

ASFENDIS KAVOUSI
1476m

To AGIOS NICHOLÁOS

EPISKOPI

PANO HORIO

MONASTERY ARKAD
Walk 14   Walk 20

A bewildering church in Episkopi has a split personality - under the Byzantine dome the Greek Orthodox community worshipped; just beside under a pitched roof was the Catholic congregation.

Soon the air is pine scented as the surrounding mountains display an array of greenery almost unbeknown to the parched rockiness of Eastern Crete. The dirt track persists between a sheer rock face and a sharply cut cleft below, before arriving at the upland valley of Thripti. (1h 40m).

The few residences of Thripti are occupied primarily during the harvest season (late summer) of the vineyards. The grapes are placed in wicker baskets and brought to the markets in their most basic form or crushed into rough local wines. Nothing is wasted as the residue of the winemaking process continues one step further when it is distilled into the ferocious and popular liquor of "raki". Time stands still as the slow rhythm of village life passes with the eventuality of the seasons. Thripti offers the last chance for a cool drink of tapped springwater, but nothing else in the way of food or drink exists.

Pass to the right of the collection of Thripti's stone houses on a road that circumvents to the ridge just behind. Looking back at the ramshackle abodes, dominated by a domed church, you will soon encounter a 4-way intersection. Turn right and pass below some abandoned houses built into the hillside above, then take the left fork

The genuine hospitality you will encounter in the Cretan countryside will never be forgotten.

in the road. Though somewhat overgrown the road passes above terraced plots. In the near distance, the hamlet of Tsamantis overlooks a sharp ravine cut into the landscape to the east. A beautiful sight! (2h).

From the previous left fork it is 15 minutes to reach a saddle overlooking Kavousi and the north coast far below. A winding cobblestone path breaks away from the road for the rather steep downgrade. While the condition of the path ranges from very good to broken down, it is obvious to the eye. In ½ hour the path reaches a small road; for the remainder of the walk either follow the road or the cobblestone shortcuts to Kavousi. Once there, choose from plenty of roadside tavernas while waiting for the bus. (4h).

21) TOURLOTI – MOCHLOS – MIRSINI

Walking Time:	Tourloti down to Mochlos 1½ hours.
	Mochlos up to Mirsini 2 hours.
Access:	Take the main north coast road in an easterly direction from Agios Nicholaos towards Sitia. After 41 kms. you will come upon the small town of Sfaka. On the west side of Sfaka there is a poor, small road leading down into Mochlos just 7 kms. away. Sfaka is located 31 kms. west of Sitia.
	Bus Journey Time: 1 hour.
	Bus service is frequent to the towns of Sfaka, Mirsini, and Tourloti on the Agios Nicholaos to Sitia (and vice-versa) run. Mochlos is a moderately short walk from any of these towns. A taxi may be hired from Mochlos up to the town of Sfaka along the main route, if a one way walk is desired.
	In summer, boats ferry visitors across the Gulf of Mirabello from Agios Nicholaos to Mochlos. Check with travel agents in Agios Nicholaos for boating arrangements.
Description:	The view is magnificent over the soft contours of the

vineyards below, with the clashing of rock cliffs to one side. The local wine lives up to its good reputation and is best served right out of the barrel ("crassi apo varelli"). Easily discernable below is the small town of Mochlos, nearly joined with the even smaller island of the same name. In the background is the inviting Gulf of Mirabello. All the ingredients for an interesting excursion in eastern Crete can be

127

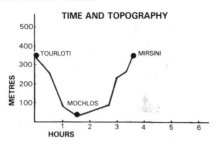

found here.

This walk may be taken in a variety of combinations, but for our purpose we will begin at the small village of Tourloti. This town appears barely to hang on the side of a mountain between still higher peaks and the sea. Follow a paved road to the back of town on the sea side. The road soon regresses to dirt and descends gradually downhill. It is infrequently used by the villagers to tend their gardens below. Follow along the main dirt track – don't be tempted by smaller side roads as shortcuts, often they are not.

The dirt road meanders downhill for about an hour before reaching a "T" intersection – to the left (west) is Mochlos. It is another ½ hour past a large new hotel complex to the charming village of Mochlos. (1½h). There are plenty of tavernas serving locally caught fish, with rooms to let and a small hotel. The island of Mochlos is within swimming distance if the walk wasn't enough to get your heart pumping. There is also the possibility of arranging for a ride over on a local fisherman's caique.

The small island was connected to present day Mochlos long ago with the slight land mass in-between forming a natural harbour. The harbour, which was accessible from either side, disappeared due to the local subsidence of this area. There is still evidence on the island of early Minoan remains. It was excavated by a young American named Richard Seager in 1907-8 (along with the nearby island just to the west called Psiras). Among the discoveries were large stone vessels used as burials and their contents. There were vases of alabaster, marble, fragile gold jewellery and some of the earliest sealstones known from Crete.

Mochlos is the perfect kind of place to spend an afternoon or an eternity. The pace is slow and while the village is just across the bay from the resort metropolis of Agios Nicholaos, it feels as if it were a world away. Though there is no beach to shout about, the small

128

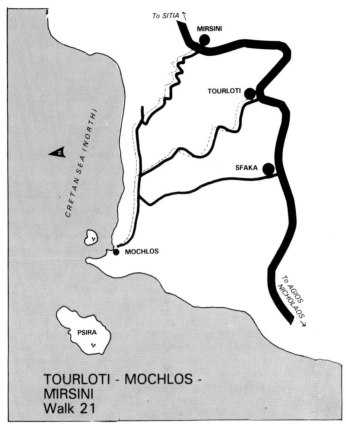

TOURLOTI - MOCHLOS -
MIRSINI
Walk 21

picturesque valley locked in at the east end by towering rock cliffs
more than compensates.

The walk back up to Mirsini from Mochlos is more strenuous to be
sure, but well worth the trip. Follow the main road out of Mochlos to
the east. It is easy to locate the small villages of Mirsini and Tourloti
above. (Tourloti sticks out on a pinnacle to the west of Mirsini.) The
first fork leads to Sfaka on a fairly well travelled road – 1 hour 15
minutes by foot, and the second to Tourloti. Stay along the low road
until practically reaching the rock cliffs. The dirt track continues
along through well maintained gardens of loquat and lemon trees,

and various types of produce. In an hour or so the road ends abruptly at a small chapel alongside a stone Venetian watchtower. This in itself is a nice country walk. (2½h).

If you are game for the climb uphill to Mirsini, backtrack about 100 metres to a road that doubles back and leads uphill from the coast. The walk will take another hour and once again the views are wonderful. Just after branching onto this road, there are nearby remnants of a Venetian fort, now topped with a small, whitewashed chapel. It is easy to assume the position of the watch, looking over the horizon for any encroaching vessels. It also happens to be a great spot for a picnic.

The road branches uphill onto a slightly larger dirt road that zig-zags through endless olive groves. Once in Mirsini, there are a couple of very small cafés in which to get a drink. Our experience here included being plied with Raki from a gourd to friendly exhortations of "Stin Yassou!" (to our health)! If the Pappas (priest) is in town he will gladly open up the main church for a quick look. It is built around a 14th century chapel, in effect entombing the older, frescoed one inside. (3½h).

22) ZAKROS – VALLEY OF THE DEAD

Walking Time: 2 hours from Ano Zakros down to Kato Zakros. 3 hours from Kato Zakros up to Ano Zakros on alternate route.

Access: Follow the coastal road out of Sitia in an easterly direction to the town of Paleokastro (19 km.). Turn due south onto a road (just after the Cathedral) that will take you to Ano Zakros 939 km.). This is where the walk begins, but there is a road that continues 7 km. down to Kato Zakros along the coast. In the summer you can probably count on getting a lift back to the top if you don't feel like making the return trip by foot.

Bus Journey Time: 1¼ hours.
There is bus service from Sitia to Ano Zakros 3 times daily until early afternoon.

Description: Truly one of the most fascinating, integral and beautiful walks on Crete is located at the eastern extreme of the island. The walk begins at the town of Ano (Upper) Zakros and leads through a ravine that is known as the "Valley of the Dead". The sides of the deep cleft rise at sheer angles from the river bed and over a

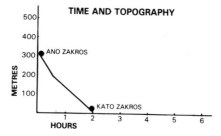

hundred caves line the upper portions. Many Minoan tombs and their contents were discovered within the caves (now on display at the Archaeological Museum in Iraklion) – hence the gruesome name. The jewel of the walk lies near the bottom of the canyon, in a theatrical hillside setting, overlooking a small bay. It is the Minoan palace at Kato (Lower) Zakros.

The walk begins somewhat inauspiciously at the town of Ano Zakros which provides the basic services of hotel, rooms to let, and a few tavernas. Follow a sign indicating Kato Zakros out of town along a paved road to the well preserved remains of some Minoan villas. From this point, it is 20 minutes more of asphalt before turning left on a dirt road that leads to the top opening of the "Valley of the Dead".

Pull aside the shepherd's makeshift gate, lock it behind, and begin the odyssey downhill, The first 20 minutes, once inside the ravine, are the most difficult. The descent is rapid and occasional rubble build up requires the use of both hands and feet to negotiate the dry stream bed. One note of caution is simply to be aware of the Angora goats that are kept in this area. Sometimes their agile feet knock loose a rock or two from above. Don't let this description scare off too many of you – after all, the going is only a bit rough for 20 minutes, and there are ample rewards below.

Soon the pitch levels out, and a good marked trail follows along the north aside of the stream bed. (1h). The red dots mark your progress for the remaining hour of the walk. The thick underbrush, shade trees and dramatic rock walls dotted with caves, place you in solitary wonderment. The flowers inside the ravine cling to a life that would be impossible elsewhere. The Dragon Arûm (see sketch) is a brilliant example of the variety of flowers that abound on Crete. The massive size of the flower made up of spathe and spadix is accentuated by its deep purple colour (March – May). At the bottom of the ravine, turn left (north) onto a small dirt road leading through thick groves of

131

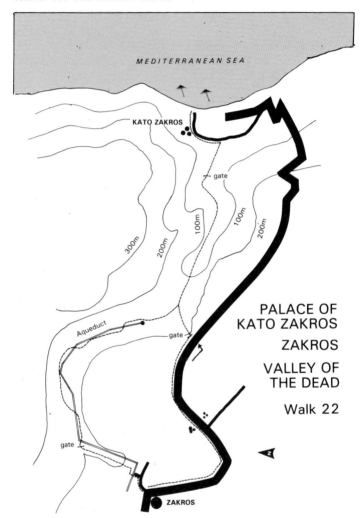

MEDITERRANEAN SEA

KATO ZAKROS

gate

100m

100m

200m

200m

300m

Aqueduct

gate

gate

ZAKROS

PALACE OF
KATO ZAKROS

ZAKROS

VALLEY OF
THE DEAD

Walk 22

banana and olive trees before reaching the site of the palace. (2h).

The palace occupies a superb position, with a port facing to the Nile Delta where the majority of its trade way was likely carried out. At the turn of the century an excavation by the British archaeologist David Hogarth turned up only a series of Minoan houses. It wasn't until 1961 that a Greek Professor, Dr. Nicholas Platon, sunk a trial trench at the site to discover the fifth Minoan palace which we call Kato Zakros. Platon tells in his book on the excavation how he immediately struck the ruins of a Minoan palace within only a few metres of Hogarth's attempt some 60 years before.

Built in the New Palatial period, the key features of Kato Zakros generally conform to the other palaces. Besides the main palace and extensive workshops, the surrounding town climbed the slopes of two nearby hills. The palace was 2 or 3 storeys tall and constructed around a central courtyard. The most distinctive feature of this palace is the cistern and well located in the east wing. Today this area can be marshy, thus providing a suitable sanctuary for a family of herons.

The palace at Kato Zakros has provided some of the richest and most interesting archaeological finds since Sir Arthur Evans excavated the palace of Knossos. The palace was never plundered, allowing the treasures inside to be found in large quantities. The storage magazines were discovered exactly as they were left, with over 50 large stone jars inside. In addition, there were literally thousands of pitchers, pots, jugs, other vessels, many metal implements and fine gold jewellery. Clay tablets with Linear A script were found in the archives.

The entire area was destroyed by fire near the end of the 15th century B.C. large stones from the palace façade were hurled great distances and the upper storeys collapsed. The debate still rages as to the exact cause of the great destruction to all of the palaces on Crete. Somehow at Kato Zakros, the people had enough warning to flee the palace very hastily and without their belongings.

There are several tavernas and some rooms to let along the small stretch of rocky beach just down from the ruins. It is a good spot for a swim and a bite to eat before the trek (on a slightly different route) back to Ano Zakros. If the area is inundated with people from tour buses, don't worry too much, they never stay long.

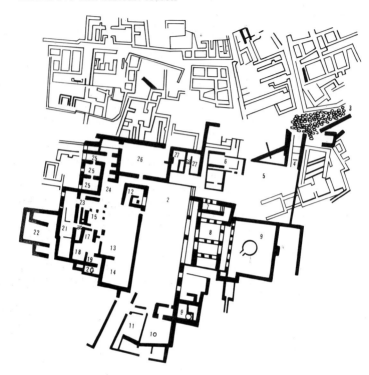

PALACE OF KATO ZAKROS

1. Central Courtyard	**WEST WING**	**NORTH WING**
2. Altar	12. Anteroom	25. Storerooms
EAST WING	13. Hall of Ceremonies	26. Kitchen
3. Entrance	14. Banquet Hall	27. Storerooms
4. Stepped Ramp	15. Priest's Room ?	28. Staircase
5. Courtyard	17. Lustral Basin	
6. Bathroom	18. Treasury	
7. King's Room	19. Workshop	
8. Queen's Room	20. Storeroom	
9. Cistern and Well	21. Archive	
SOUTH WING	22. Dye House/Workshop	
10. Sitting Room	23. Staircase to Upper Floor	
11. Workshop	24. Lobby	

Optional return to Ano Zakros:
There is a slightly longer variation for the walk back up the ravine
that we can recommend. The ascent to the top is more gradual along
the entire route. (It is possible to take this walk from the top as well,
but the trailhead is quite difficult to locate from Ano Zakros. A local
guide may provide some help for those who are interested.) Simply
follow the red dots that mark the trail inside, up to the point where
you made the rather steep descent before. This occurs 1 hour and 15
minutes into the ravine. Instead of going back the same way, follow
the marked trail to the right inside of the main canyon.

In about 15 minutes, the trail meets a still functioning aqueduct.
This concrete chute can serve as a loose guideline for the trail during
the remainder of the way. The trail seldom stays in the creekbed from
here. From the beginning of the aqueduct it takes a half hour along a
gradual incline to a shepherd's makeshift fence. Rather than
clambering over at the level of the stream bed, pass through a
makeshift gate just above. Only a couple of minutes after passing
through the gate, the trail splits – follow the left fork up a minor artery
towards Ano Zakros. It is 15 minutes along a shaded trail to the
opening of the ravine and a fine view of Ano Zakros. From the top,
the trail passes through some fenced-in pastures (look for red flags
identifying the gates) and on to the town. (3h).

APPENDIX

USEFUL GREEK

a=ah; e=eh; i=e; o=oh

Greetings and Everyday Words

Hello and Goodbye (Sing., Informal) . . . Yiá Sou
Hello and Goodbye (Pl., Formal) . . . Yiá Sas
Good Morning . . . Kalí Méra
Good Afternoon . . . Kalí Spera
Goodnight . . . Kali Níkta
How are you? (Sing., Informal) . . . Ti kánis?
How are you? (Sing., Formal) . . . Ti kánate?
Well, thank you . . . Kalá efharistó
Okay . . . Endáxi
Yes . . . Ne
No . . . Ohi (Oshi – Cretan)
Please . . . Parakaló
Thank you . . . Efharistó
Excuse me . . . Signómi
You're welcome . . . Parakaló
I understand . . . Katalavéno
I don't understand . . . Then Katalavéno
Come here! . . . Éla!
Food . . . Fagitó
Water . . . Neró
Beautiful . . . Oréos
Slow/Fast . . . Síga/Grígora
Easy/Difficult . . . Éfkolos/Dískolos
Car . . . Aftonkinitó
Bus . . . Leoforío
Ferry boat . . . Feri bot
On foot . . . Me ta Pothía

Questions

Where is (are) . . . ? . . . Pou íne . . . ?
Is there . . . ? . . . Ipárhi . . .
When? . . . Póte?
What? . . . Ti?
Which? . . . Piós?

How far is . . .? . . . Póso makriá íne . . .?
How much does it cost? . . . Póso káni?
Do you have . . .? . . . Éhete . . .?
Do you speak English? . . . Miláte Anglicá?

Time
Minute . . . Lepto
Hour . . . Óra
Day . . . Méra
Week . . . Evthomáda
Tomorrow . . . Ávrio
Early/Late . . . Norís/Argá

Weather
Hot/Cold . . . Zésti/Krío
Foggy . . . Omíli
Rain . . . Vrohí
Snow . . . Hióni
Wind . . . éhres
How will the weather be tomorrow? . . . Ti keró tha káni ávrio?
The weather is good (bad) . . . To kerós íne kalós (kakos).
Will it rain today? . . . Tha vréxi símera?

Directions
Left . . . Aristerá
Right . . . Theksiá
Straight . . . Efthía
To, Towards . . . Prós
From . . . Apó
Between . . . Metaksí
Up/Down . . . Páno/Káto
Near/Far . . . Kondá/Makriá
Here/There . . . Ethó/Ekí
After/Before . . . Metá/Prín
Eastwards . . . Anatoliká
Westwards . . . Thitiká
Northwards . . . Vória
Southwards . . . Nótia

Geography and Landmarks
Mountain . . . Vounó
Ravine . . . Farángi
River . . . Potámi
Cave . . . Spiliá
Sea . . . Thálassa
Beach . . . Paralía
Spring Water . . . Pigí
Road . . . Drómos
Footpath . . . Monopáti
Church . . . Eklisía
House . . . Spíti
Building . . . Ktírio
Village . . . Horió

A shepherds' mitato on the Nida Plateau, is built from stone in the style of an igloo.

A Sfakiot shepherd tends his flocks on the upland Askifou Plateau. He is dressed in black as a proud symbol of mourning. (Walk 10).

Emergency
Help! . . . Voíthia!
Doctor . . . Giatrós
I'm lost . . . Háthika

EMERGENCY NUMBERS

Area Code	City	Police	Hospital	Tourist Office
081	Iraklion	100	237546 or, 237524	228225
0831	Rethymnon	100	27814-19	29148 or, 24143
0821	Hania	100	27231	26426
0841	Ag. Nicholaos	100		
0843	Sitia	100		
0822	Kastelli	100		
0842	Ierapetra	100		

SELECTED BIBLIOGRAPHY

Bowman, John, *A Traveller's Guide to Crete*, Jonathan Cape, London, new and revised edition, 1985.

Cameron, Pat, *The Blue Guide to Crete*, A. & C. Black, London, Fourth Edition 1986.

Clark, Alan, *The Fall of Crete*, Blond, London, 1962. Nel Mentor, 1969.

Davaras, Costis, *Guide to Cretan Antiquities*, NOYES Press, Park Ridge, NJ, 1976.

Felding, Xan, *The Stronghold*, Seeker and Warburg, London, 1954.

Graves, Robert, *The Greek Myths*, 2 Vols., Penguin, London, 1957.

Herzfeld, Michael, *The Poetics of Manhood*, Princeton University Press, Princeton, 1985.

Homer, *The Iliad*, translated by E. V. Rieu, Penguin, London, 1950.

Homer, *The Odyssey*, translated by E. V. Rieu, Penguin, London, 1946.

Hopkins, Adam, *Crete, Its Past, Present and People*, Faber and Faber, 1983.

Iatridis, Yanoukos, *Flowers of Crete*, published by the author, Athens, 1985.

Kazantzakis, Nikos, *Zorba*, Faber Paperbacks, London, 1961.

Kazantzakis, Nikos, *Freedom or Death*, Faber Paperbacks, London, 1966.

Pashley, Robert, *Travels in Crete*, 2 Vols., Cambridge, 1837.

Pendlebury, J. D. S., *The Archaeology of Crete, An Introduction*, Metheun, London, 1939.

Platon, Nicholas, *Crete*, Nagel, Geneva, 1966.

Polunin and Huxley, *Flowers in the Mediterranean*, Chatto and Windus, 1967.

Powell, Dilys, *The Villa Ariadne*, Hodder and Stoughton, London, 1973.

Psychoundakis, George, *The Cretan Runner*, John Murray, London, 1955.

Smith, Michael Llewellyn, *The Great Island, A Study of Crete*, Longmans, London, 1965.

Spratt, Captain T. A. B., *Travels and Researched in Crete*, 2 Vols., London, 1865.

Sakellarakis, J. A., *Heraklion Museum*, Ekdothike, Athens, 1985.

Trevor-Battys, Aubyn, *Camping in Crete*, Witherby & Co., 1913.

Tournefort, Joseph de, *A Voyage into the Levant*, London, 1718.

CICERONE PRESS BOOKS

Cicerone publish a range of guides to walking and climbing in Britain

LAKE DISTRICT
LAKELAND VILLAGES
WORDSWORTH'S DUDDON
  REVISITED
REFLECTIONS ON THE LAKES
THE WESTMORLAND HERITAGE
  WALK
THE HIGH FELLS OF LAKELAND
IN SEARCH OF WESTMORLAND
CONISTON COPPER MINES
  A Field Guide
CONISTON COPPER A History
SCRAMBLES IN THE LAKE
  DISTRICT
WINTER CLIMBS IN THE LAKE
  DISTRICT
THE REGATTA MEN
LAKELAND A taste to Remember.
  (Recipes)
THE CHRONICLES OF
  MILNTHORPE
WALKS IN SILVERDALE/
  ARNSIDE Area of Outstanding
  Natural Beauty
BIRDS OF MORECAMBE BAY

NORTHERN ENGLAND
THE YORKSHIRE DALES
LAUGHS ALONG THE PENNINE
  WAY (Cartoons)
THE RIBBLE WAY
NORTH YORK MOORS
WALKING THE CLEVELAND
  WAY AND MISSING LINK
WALKS ON THE WEST PENNINE
  MOORS
WALKING NORTHERN
  RAILWAYS Vol 1. East
  Vol 2. West
BIRDS OF MERSEYSIDE
ROCK CLIMBS IN LANCASHIRE
  AND THE NORTH WEST
THE ISLE OF MAN COASTAL
  PATH

DERBYSHIRE PEAK DISTRICT
WHITE PEAK WALKS Vol 1 & 2
HIGH PEAK WALKS
WHITE PEAK WAY
KINDER LOG

WALES
THE RIDGES OF SNOWDONIA
HILL WALKING IN SNOWDONIA
ASCENT OF SNOWDON
WELSH WINTER CLIMBS

WELSH BORDER
ROCK CLIMBS IN THE WEST
  MIDLANDS

SOUTH & WEST ENGLAND
WALKS IN KENT
THE WEALDWAY & VANGUARD
  WAY
THE SOUTH DOWNS WAY &
  DOWNS LINK
WALKING ON DARTMOOR
SOUTH WEST WAY Vol 1 and 2

SCOTLAND
SCRAMBLES IN LOCHABER
SCRAMBLES IN SKYE
ROCK CLIMBS: GLEN NEVIS &
  LOCHABER OUTCROPS
THE ISLAND OF RHUM
CAIRNGORMS, WINTER CLIMBS
WINTER CLIMBS BEN NEVIS &
  GLENCOE
SCOTTISH RAILWAY WALKS

*Also a full range of guide
books to walking, scrambling,
ice-climbing, rock climbing,
and other adventurous
pursuits in Britain and
abroad.*

*Available from bookshops, outdoor equipment shops or direct
(send for price list) from: CICERONE PRESS, 2 POLICE SQUARE,
MILNTHORPE, CUMBRIA LA7 7PY*

Printed by Carnmor Print & Design,
95/97, London Road, Preston, Lancashire.